Visualize Your Vocabulary

Turn Any SAT/ACT Word into a Picture and Remember It Forever

Volume 3

Shayne Gardner

To God . . . for His grace, blessings, and answered prayers.

The limits of my language are the limits of my mind. All I know is what I have words for. — Ludwig Wittgenstein

Copyright © 2017

Visualize Your Vocabulary: Turn Any SAT/ACT Word into a Picture and Remember It Forever, Volume 3

By Shayne Gardner

Illustrations: Kris Hagen

Editing: Sarah Wolbach

All rights reserved. No part of this book may be reproduced in any form or transmitted by any means without written permission from the publisher.

* SAT is a registered trademark of the College Entrance Examination Board, which does not endorse this book.

* ACT is a registered trademark of ACT, Inc., which does not endorse this book.

Library of Congress Catalog Card Number:

ISBN-13: 978-1981332106

ISBN-10: 1981332103

Printed by CreateSpace

Facebook.com/VisualizeYourVocabulary

Pinterest.com/SATwerdnerd

Twitter.com/SATwerdnerd

Google.com/+VisualizeYourVocabulary

VisualizeYourVocabulary@gmail.com

Table of Contents

Introduction……………………………………………………..vi
Vocabulary Words……………………………………………...1
Index………………………………………………………….253

Introduction

Why this book?

If you read *Visualize Your Vocabulary* and use this mnemonic aid for other SAT and ACT words not included here, you will gain a remarkable edge over students who do not. You will ingest the academic equivalent of steroids for an athlete.

The rationale for this book is simple. We think in pictures. Studies show most people are visual learners. The brain remembers pictures better than words. So if you want to learn new words as fast as possible, and actually enjoy the process, turn your words into pictures and skip the rote memorization.

Who should read this book?

Anyone who wants to expand their vocabulary should study this book. Moreover, because all of the 250 vocabulary words in each volume of *Visualize Your Vocabulary* are SAT and ACT words, the book is an invaluable resource for students preparing to take these or other standardized college entrance exams. It can also be extremely helpful for learning-disabled students, whether they are college-bound or not.

How it works

The simple trick of turning a word into a picture is called a mnemonic. We have used this memory technique from early childhood without knowing it. For example, we used pictures to learn the words to the nursery rhyme "Twinkle, Twinkle, Little Star." Mnemonics can be used to learn anything from algebraic formulas and history to grammar rules.

My favorite memory technique is converting the abstract definition of a word into a concrete "thing" that I can visualize in my mind's eye. Many times a difficult word I want to memorize doesn't want to stick. However, if I take the time to turn it into a picture, it sticks like Super Glue, and I never forget it.

The trick is to come up with something familiar to you that rhymes with the word you want to learn. This rhyming word serves as the link, or bridge, between the word and the definition. I call this linking word the "memory word." Next, you turn the definition into a picture that includes the memory word. As an example, take the noun *alacrity*, which means "cheerful eagerness or readiness to respond; liveliness." My memory word is "a-black-kitty," a near perfect rhyme. My picture for *alacrity* is:

> When you return home after a long day at school, your unusual pet, **a black kitty, cheerfully and eagerly** runs out to greet you. He is six feet tall and can walk on his hind legs. He does a few somersaults, grabs your backpack with a smile on his face, and carries it for you. Once inside the house, he pulls off your shoes, puts your slippers on your feet, cartwheels into the kitchen to pour your favorite drink, and then lies down purring at your feet.

It's that simple. I used the rhyming word "a-black-kitty" to link the vocabulary word and the action picture that describes it. Now, whenever I hear or see the word *alacrity*, I think of what it sounds like, visualize the picture, and the definition comes flooding into my mind.

Rules of the game

A few simple rules make the picture stick like glue. If you don't use these rules when creating your picture, you will certainly find it too boring and bland. Boring won't work, and you will forget the word.

Rule #1   Make the picture impossible, crazy, and illogical. In my picture for *alacrity*, the kitty is six feet tall, walks on his hind legs, carries a backpack, and does somersaults and cartwheels. Impossible! If the picture's scenario is possible or too logical, it will be difficult to remember the word. Crazy jumps out at you, and you easily remember it.

Rule #2   Action! This is often incorporated with Rule #1, but it must be emphasized. The more movement and action you put into your picture, the more your mind's eye will notice it. This is similar to how we perceive movement with our peripheral vision. In my example for *alacrity*, "cheerfully and eagerly" is depicted with an abundance of action.

Rule #3   Personalize the picture to increase retention. If you insert yourself, a family member, or a close friend into the picture, you will be much more likely to remember it.

Rule #4   Exaggerate size and number. If an insect graces your picture, make it the size of a human, or even King Kong. A million insects might be better than just one. Remember, the kitty in *alacrity* is an abnormal size, standing six feet tall.

Rule #5   Use all five senses. If it stinks, make it reek so badly that you can feel your nose hairs curl up. If it smells good, make it euphoric. If you can hear it, amplify the sound. Taste it. Is it bitter, sweet, sour, or spicy? If it hits you, make it really hurt; maybe it gives you a bloody nose.

Rule #6   Add color. Who says that blood has to be red? That is too normal and logical. You will more easily remember the impossibility of blue or hot pink blood pouring out of your nose.

The common denominator for all of these rules is "nonsensical." Anything goes. The more impossible you make it, the better; the only limit is your imagination.

The format of this book

For each vocabulary word in the book, I provide the pronunciation, indicate its part of speech (noun, verb, etc.), define it, list several synonyms, and use it in a sentence. Some words can function as more than one part of speech. Many times, a word has multiple nuanced definitions; if so, I try to use the most common definitions. You will notice a theme with the sentences. If a sample sentence doesn't immediately come to mind as I am writing, I gleefully launch a salvo into the stereotypical politician's camp. I thoroughly enjoy goring that ox!

More than half of all English words stem from Latin, and many have Greek origins. If a word has a Latin origin, I point that out; if I find another origin interesting, I mention that as well. I have discovered that about 90 percent of SAT and ACT vocabulary words stem from Latin, and a few stem from Greek. Hence, my omission of most origins apart from these languages.

After all of the boring stuff, the fun begins. I provide the memory word and the action picture, followed by a snapshot illustration of the action picture, drawn by the wonderful artist Kris Hagen.

Use your creativity!

I strive to come up with a memory word that rhymes as closely as possible with the vocabulary word. I am not always completely satisfied with what comes to mind, but I do the best I can. You may come up with a better rhyming word and consequently a better picture. If so, use your mnemonic instead of mine.

Have fun, and look for more volumes of *Visualize Your Vocabulary* in the near future.

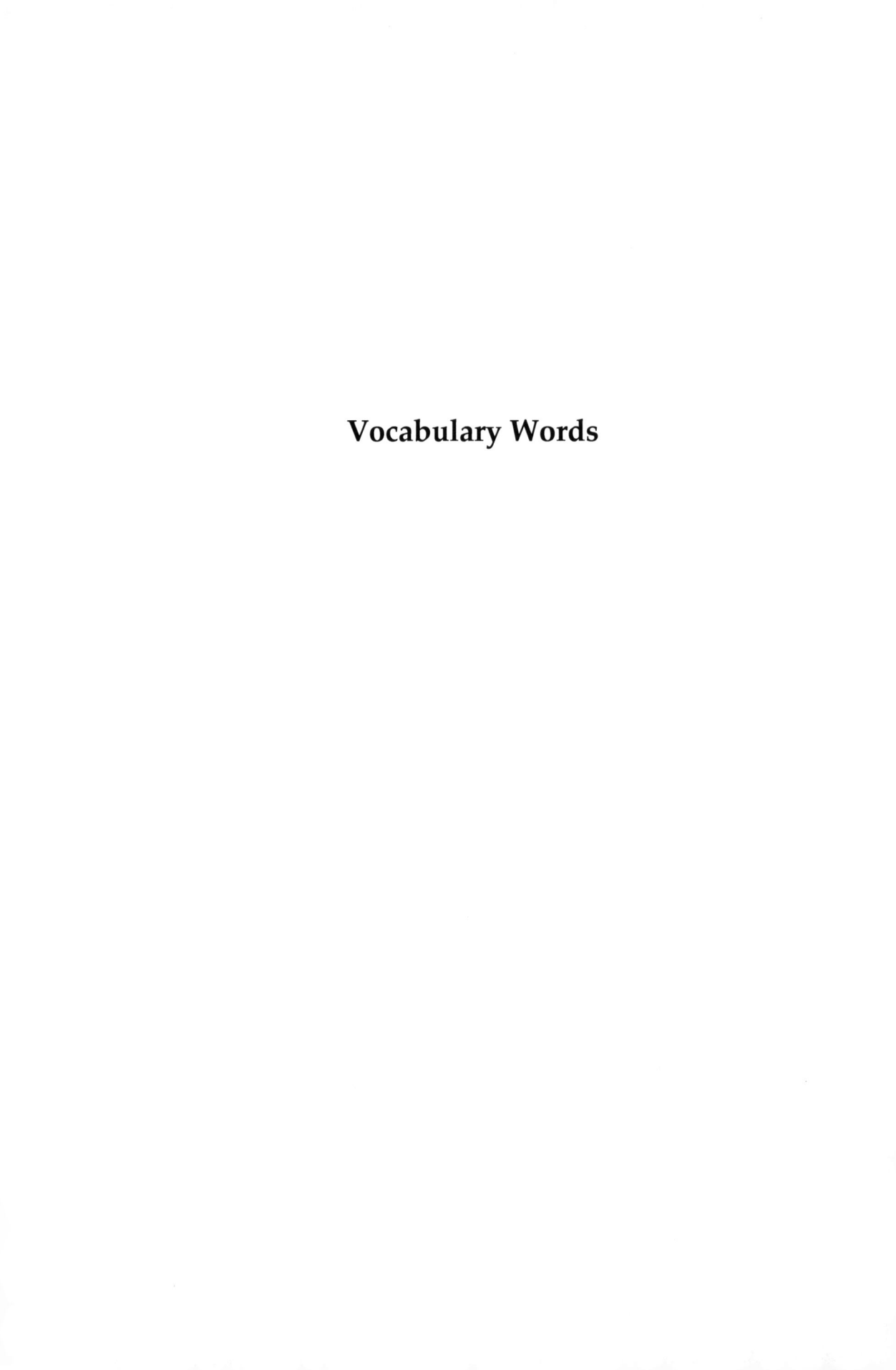

Vocabulary Words

antagonist: (an-**tag**-uh-nist) **noun** – a person who is opposed to, struggles against, or competes with another

synonyms: adversary, enemy, foe, opponent, rival

origin: From the Latin *antagonista*, meaning "competitor, opponent."

example: Even great presidents, such as George Washington, Abraham Lincoln, and Calvin Coolidge, had their **antagonists**.

memory word: Aunt-Agnes

picture: *Aunt Agnes* takes the opposite side of every issue. She likes to play devil's advocate and *oppose* everything anyone says.

spontaneous: (spon-**tay**-nee-uhs) **adjective** – said or done without being planned or written in advance

synonyms: extemporaneous, impromptu, on the fly, unplanned

origin: From the Latin *sponte*, meaning "of one's own accord."

example: The phenomenon of **spontaneous** combustion fascinates me.

memory word: Spartan-Aeneas (ih-**nee**-uhs)

picture: Unlike other Spartans, Aeneas does everything *on the fly*. (Sparta was a military state that emphasized physical fitness and military training to create ultimate warriors.) He never thinks anything through before leaping into action. When news arrives that a neighboring city-state has been bad-mouthing the Spartans, Aeneas grabs his spear and sword, yelling, "Let's march on them and cut off their heads!" The Spartan leader objects: "Hold on! Not so fast, **Spartan Aeneas**. Let's talk this through before we act."

adroit: (uh-**droit**) **adjective** – expert or nimble in physical activity, or in handling difficult people or situations

synonyms: adept, apt, artful, clever, deft, dexterous, savvy, skillful

example: James Bond is the epitome of an **adroit** man in action.

memory word: a-droid

picture: An amazing Las Vegas show features *a droid*. During a performance, a suicide bomber stands up in the front row and threatens to blow the place up. The droid, programmed to *handle difficult situations skillfully*, talks the man down, disarms the bomb, and restrains him until the police arrive — all while juggling a chainsaw, a flaming torch, a bowling ball, and a squealing pig.

hamper: (**ham**-per) **verb** – to hinder, impede, or interfere with the progress of something

synonyms: encumber, frustrate, handicap, inconvenience, obstruct

example: The persistent rain **hampered** the progress of construction throughout the metropolitan area.

memory word: hamper (clothes hamper)

picture: A long, slow-moving train hauling humongous *hamper*s on flatbed cars *impedes* traffic at the railroad crossing.

terse: (turs) **adjective** – of few words; brief and to the point

synonyms: brusque, concise, curt, laconic, pithy, pointed, succinct

origin: From the Latin *tersus*, meaning "clean, neat, scrupulous."

example: Most of the tough-guy characters in the movie *The Expendables* are **terse**. They only speak when absolutely necessary.

memory word: tears

picture: Grandpa says few words and ***gets to the point.*** He says to his granddaughter, who is crying and experiencing a very emotional event, "*Tears* help." What he means is "That's right, cry it all out. Cry until you can't cry anymore. *Tears* are magically cathartic. After a good cry, you will feel much better."

banal: (buh-**nal**) **adjective** – lacking freshness or originality

synonyms: bland, common, ho-hum, insipid, mundane, ordinary, trite

example: The student's presentation on the history of cardboard was **banal**.

memory word: flannel

picture: A grunge dude, getting dressed for the day, opens his closet, which contains nothing but denim jeans and assorted *flannel* shirts. His *boring* wardrobe is *lacking freshness and originality*.

minutia: (mi-**noo**-shuh) **noun** – precise details; small matters

synonyms: fine points, trifles, trivia, triviality

example: Devoted *Star Trek* fans love to tuck little nuggets of Trekkie **minutia** into the dark corners of their minds, ready for recall at a moment's notice.

memory word: Medusa

picture: Before signing a lengthy contract, **Medusa** reads the large print while the snakes on her head closely scrutinize the ***details in small print***.

egregious: (ih-**gree**-juhs) **adjective** – extremely bad

synonyms: deplorable, grievous, heinous, nefarious, reprehensible

origin: From the Latin *egregious*, meaning "distinguished, excellent."

example: Somewhere along the way, the meaning of **egregious** made a 180 degree turn for the worse.

memory word: a-green-juice

picture: An *extremely bad* guy is on work release at Jumbo Juice. Every time a customer orders ***a green juice***, a mischievous Cheshire grin transforms his face. He proceeds to empty his sinuses into the mix . . . if you know what I mean. Then he scrapes some fungus from between his toes, adding it to the smoothie. He maintains the creepy grin as he hands it to the customer, commenting, "Enjoy your drink and have a nice day."

proclivity: (proh-**kliv**-i-tee) **noun** – a natural tendency or inclination

synonyms: bias, cup of tea, penchant, predilection, propensity

origin: From the Latin *proclivis*, meaning "prone to, inclined."

example: Phido has a **proclivity** to hang his head out the window of the car, no matter how fast dad drives.

memory word: broke-levity

picture: Downer Dave strolled over where his friends sat yucking it up, having a good time. His ***strong inclination toward*** depression threw a wet blanket on their fun and ***broke*** the ***levity***.

detrimental: (de-truh-**men**-tl) **adjective** – causing harm or damage

synonyms: baleful, deleterious, destructive, pernicious

origin: From the Latin *detrimentum*, meaning "loss, damage."

example: Plagiarism can be **detrimental** to your grade.

memory word: Debra-mental

picture: Debra resides in a padded room. She wears a white jacket with extra-long sleeves to keep her from *harming* herself. *Debra* is *mental*.

abhor: (ab-**hawr**) **verb** – to find repugnant; to detest utterly

synonyms: despise, hate, loathe

origin: From the Latin's *abhorrere*, meaning "to shrink back from, wince."

example: Many of us **abhor** texting while driving.

memory word: app-hoard

picture: A man has hundreds of apps on his smartphone, way more than he will ever use. It takes the *app hoard*er forever to find the app he wants, and he has to reboot his phone several times a day. Consequently, he now *utterly detests* his phone. He throws it at a brick wall, and it explodes into thousands of pieces and app shrapnel flies in every direction.

forlorn: (fawr-**lawrn**) **adjective** – miserable, lonely, and sad

synonyms: bereft, despondent, disconsolate, forsaken, hopeless

example: If Werdnerd were the last man on Earth, he would be at peace if he had a stack of dictionaries. Without them, he would be **forlorn**.

memory word: four-Laurens

picture: *Four Laurens*, stranded on a deserted island, collapse onto the beach, *miserable* and *despondent*.

prescient: (**presh**-uhnt) **adjective** – having knowledge of events before they occur

synonyms: clairvoyant, foresighted, intuitive, prophetic, psychic

origin: From the Latin *praescire*, meaning "to know in advance."

example: If you predict the winning lottery numbers, yet fail to purchase a lottery ticket, you are both **prescient** and stupid.

memory word: present

picture: A little girl has many birthday *present*s. She holds each wrapped *present* up to her ear and gently shakes it. She then announces the contents. Everyone wonders how her *foresight* can be 100 percent accurate.

lithe: (lahyth) **adjective** – moving or bending with ease

synonyms: agile, flexible, limber, loose, nimble, pliable, supple

example: What do ballerinas, snakes, and cats have in common? They are all **lithe**.

memory word: lite (beer)

picture: A can of Sud *Lite* beer shows off its *flexibility* by performing a back bend.

aptitude: (**ap**-ti-tood) **noun** – innate or acquired talent for something; readiness or easiness in learning

synonyms: ability, bent, disposition, leaning, proclivity, propensity

origin: From the Latin *aptitudo*, meaning "fitness."

example: The Scholastic **Aptitude** Test (SAT) is designed to measure a student's **aptitude** or readiness for college.

memory word: apple-toot

picture: An apple demonstrates its superior *ability* while taking the SAT. It whizzes through the exam, whistling all the while. No one notices because the apple flatulates throughout the exam and everyone, including the proctor, lies unconscious from the *apple toots*.

vitriolic: (vi-tree-**ol**-ik) **adjective** – very caustic or scathing

synonyms: acerbic, antagonistic, biting, cutting, harsh, mordant, sharp

example: The media bombards some politicians with **vitriolic** scorn while treating others with fawning admiration.

memory word: victory-olic

picture: Imagine one of those dads who wants his son to win at all costs. He's addicted to victory. After his son is tagged out at third base, the *victoryolic* dad shouts some *harsh and caustic* words at the umpire.

loathsome: (lohth-sum) **adjective** – highly offensive; arousing disgust

synonyms: abhorrent, detestable, odious, repugnant, repulsive, revolting

example: Bill Clinton wrote a letter to Colonel Eugene Holmes in 1969, explaining in detail why he found the U.S. military **loathsome**. That same Bill Clinton became the Commander in Chief of the U.S. military in 1993 when he became president.

memory word: loaf-some

picture: A *repulsive* school lunch lady serves the same *disgusting* meal every Friday: meatloaf made from mystery meat and all of the week's leftovers. She plops the *abominable* garbage on each student's tray as they file by, saying to each one, "Here's the meat *loaf some* love, and some hate. No seconds allowed. Move along!"

peevish: (**pee**-vish) **adjective** – showing annoyance or irritation

synonyms: cantankerous, crabby, cranky, grouchy, pertinacious, petulant

example: Loss of sleep can make anyone **peevish**.

memory word: pee-fish

picture: The fish in the aquarium are *annoyed and irritated* at one particular fish they call *pee-fish*. Why? He thinks he's a dog, so he swims around hiking his hind fin, peeing on stuff.

equivocate: (ih-**kwiv**-uh-kayt) **verb** – to be deliberately vague, ambiguous, or unclear in order to mislead or deceive

synonyms: dodge, evade, hem and haw, prevaricate, tergiversate

example: If I were more diplomatic, I would say politicians merely **equivocate**. Instead, I say they lie, cheat, and steal to obtain and maintain power.

memory word: a-quiver-cake

picture: Little Werdnerd is up to it again. (See "prevaricate," vol. 2.) This time, mom makes *a quiver cake* for her kids. It's a Jell-O cake covered with icing. Entering the kitchen, she notices a slice missing and Werdnerd, one of her three boys, busily licking his fingers. She asks if he ate some cake without permission and he **dodges,** *"I'm not saying I did and I'm not saying I didn't."* He'll make a good politician someday.

fractious: (frak-shuhs) **adjective** – easily irritated or annoyed; unruly

synonyms: intractable, peevish, petulant, querulous, stubborn

example: Spirit was an indomitable and **fractious** horse that would not submit to harness and saddle.

memory word: fractions

picture: You are *easily irritated* doing your math homework, especially when working with *fractions.* Those **stubborn, unruly fractions** jump off the page, refusing to behave. They create bedlam on your desktop.

dissonant: (**dis**-uh-nuhnt) **adjective** – out of harmony; not in accord

synonyms: cacophonous, discordant, grating, incompatible, incongruous

origin: From the Latin *dissonare*, meaning "to differ in sound."

example: A politician's actions and words are quite often **dissonant**.

memory word: dis-an-ant

picture: The ants vie with the mosquitoes during the Friday night football game. The ant fans perform their favorite chant, "Red ant, black ant, yellow ant, blue. You're all great, and we love you!" Immediately after this cheer, a mosquito in their midst, ***not in accord*** with them, yells, "Ants suck!" It is smart enough to take flight immediately after it ***diss***es ***an ant***.

irrelevant: (ih-**rel**-uh-vuhnt) **adjective** – not applicable or pertinent

synonyms: beside the point, immaterial, off the topic, unrelated

example: Two of my friends are twins. One always has something apropos to say for every occasion. The other never makes any sense; everything he says is **irrelevant**.

memory word: deer-elephant

picture: A deer and an elephant engage in a philosophical discussion. The deer strays from the topic and the elephant insists, "Well, that's **beside the point**. It's neither here nor there." What do you imagine the *deer elephant* conversation to be?

burnish: (**bur**-nish) **verb** – to polish by friction and make shiny

synonyms: buff, furbish, rub, shine, smoothen, wax

example: Let no man besmirch your character. **Burnish** it with the virtues of *verum, pulchrum, et bonum*— truth, beauty, and goodness.

memory word: furnish

picture: A clean freak furnishes her apartment with nothing but metal and glass. She spends all day meticulously polishing everything until it *sparkles and shines*. Obviously, she doesn't have any children.

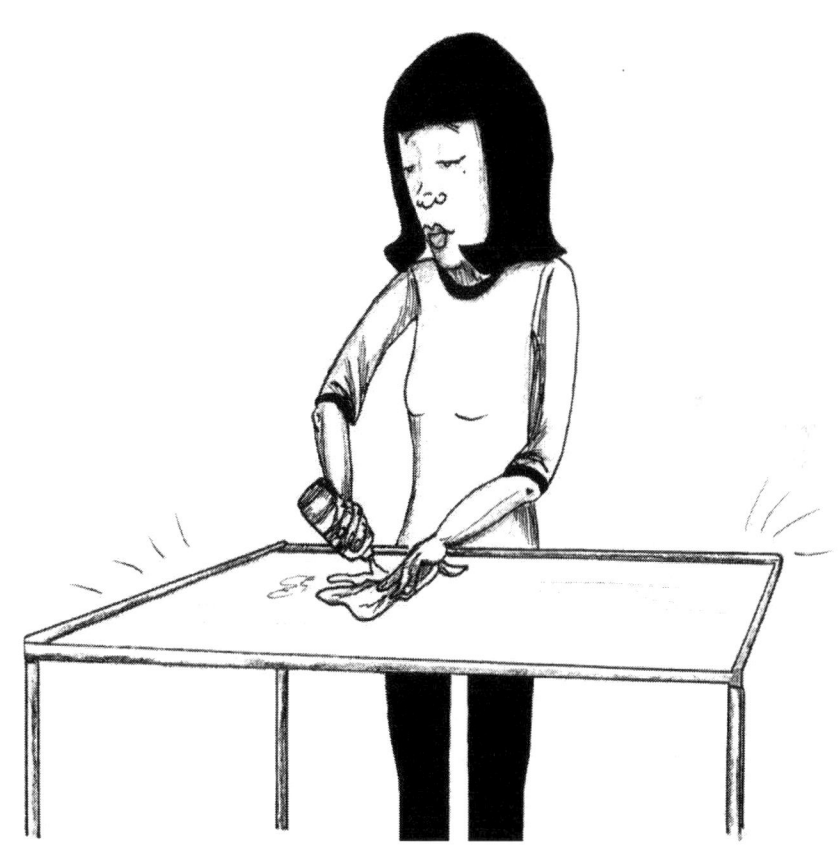

derisive: (dih-**rahy**-siv, -**ris**-iv) **adjective** – expressing contempt

synonyms: disdainful, mocking, ridiculing, rude, scornful, smart-alecky

origin: From the Latin *deridere*, meaning "to ridicule."

example: Little **derisive** Werdnerd contemptuously heckles his English teacher, saying, "Mrs. Richardson, you've got to be kidding me. You don't know the meaning of that word? Not knowing its etymology is one thing, but . . . sheesh."

memory word: dirt-icing

picture: Billy the bully observes the other students giving their teacher apples and chocolates every day. Sickened by this display of fawning, Billy decides to give her a cupcake she will never forget. It has the semblance of chocolate icing; however, after she takes a bite, she realizes Billy is *mocking* her and the other students by serving up *dirt icing.*

garrulous: (gar-uh-luhs) **adjective** – excessively talkative, usually about trivial matters

synonyms: chatty, gabby, loquacious, prolix, verbose

origin: From the Latin *garrire*, meaning "to chatter."

example: Poor Werdnerd was stuck sitting next to the most **garrulous** person on the plane.

memory word: gorillas

picture: A group of *gorillas* enjoys adult beverages during happy hour. Each one *talks nonstop.*

acrimony: (ak-ruh-moh-nee) **noun** – bitter speech or behavior

synonyms: acerbity, animosity, harshness, malice, rancor, resentment

origin: From the Latin *acrimonia,* meaning "sharpness or pungency."

example: The crowd filled with **acrimony** as the pompous senator spun lie after lie.

memory word: angry-money

picture: Several bills and coins are in a shouting and shoving match. They are a motley crew of *angry money*.

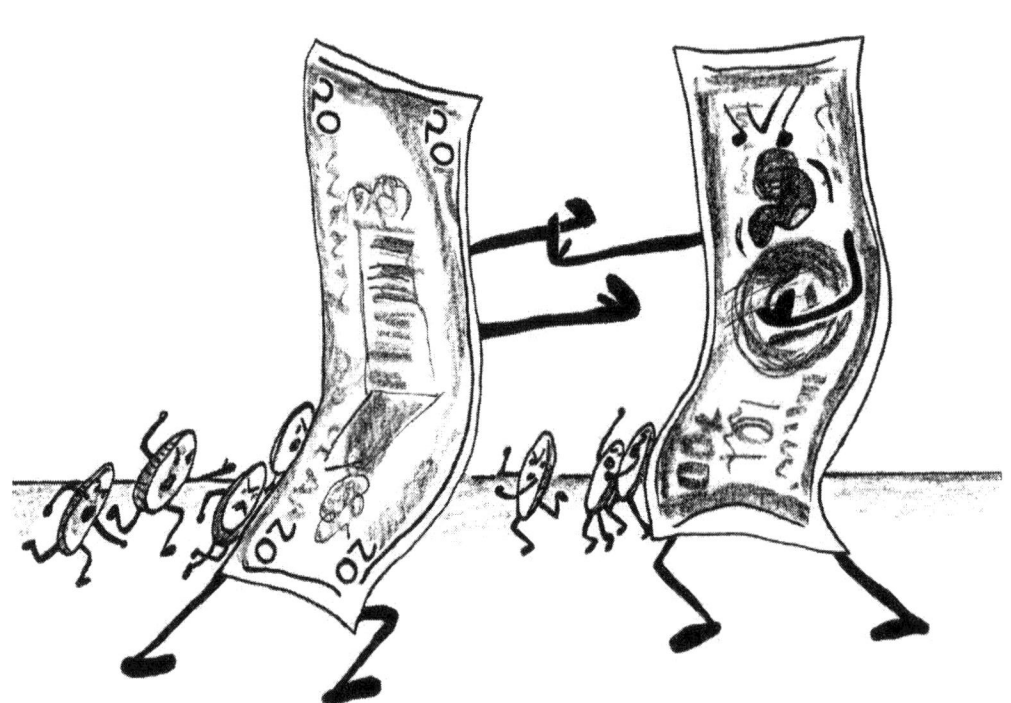

seditious: (si-**dish**-uhs) **adjective** – arousing to active opposition or rebellion against lawful authority or government

synonyms: anarchistic, defiant, factious, insurgent, mutinous, riotous

origin: From the Latin *seditiosus*, meaning "full of discord, factious, mutinous."

example: England's King George III considered the American colonies' *Declaration of Independence* a **seditious** act of war.

memory word: said-dishes

picture: A dishwasher and a chef take pride in their work at the restaurant. A waiter, who dislikes the owner, tries to ***stir up a revolt*** against her. The waiter says to the dishwasher and chef, "The boss ***said dishes*** were filthy, and the food was disgusting. Are you two going to stand for that?"

braggadocio: (brag-uh-**doh**-shee-oh) **noun** – empty boasting; bragging

synonyms: blowhard, boaster, rhodomontade, show-off, windbag

example: A **braggadocio** is someone who not only brags, but also lies about what they are bragging. For example, the braggadocio at the gym told me he could bench press 500 pounds. When I challenged him to show me, he said he benched yesterday and was too sore.

memory word: bragging-doe-seal

picture: A doe and a seal are *bragging* to each other. The seal says, "I could swim to China and back if I wanted." The doe retorts, "Oh yeah? I can run faster than you can swim, and I just ran to China and back yesterday." The *bragging doe* and *seal* go on like this all day.

supercilious: (soo-per-**sil**-ee-uhs) **adjective** – having or showing arrogant superiority and disdain

synonyms: condescending, contemptuous, haughty, imperious

origin: From the Latin *supercilium*, meaning "haughty demeanor, pride."

example: Opening the door, the butler gave me a **supercilious** up-and-down look, then turned his nose up and said, "Follow me."

memory word: soup-or-seal-guts?

picture: A couple dines at a vegetarian restaurant. She is wearing a fur coat, and he is sporting a pair of expensive alligator cowboy boots. The *condescending* waiter arrives and *disdainfully* asks, "Would you like *soup or seal guts?*"

insolent: (**in**-suh-luhnt) **adjective** – boldly rude or disrespectful

synonyms: brassy, brazen, disdainful, impertinent, insubordinate

origin: From the Latin *insolentem,* meaning "arrogant, immoderate."

example: The high school principal addressed the incoming freshmen, informing them that **insolent** behavior would not be tolerated.

memory word: insulin

picture: A *rude and disrespectful* jerk approaches an obese person placing an order in a pastry shop and asks, "Hey tubby. Just how much *insulin* do you have to inject into those thunder thighs every day?"

rambunctious: (ram-**buhngk**-shuhs) **adjective** – difficult to control or handle; lacking in restraint or discipline

synonyms: boisterous, noisy, raucous, rough, rowdy, unruly

example: When my dog was younger, she was **rambunctious,** but in her sunset years, she sleeps most of the day.

memory word: ram-bump-shins

picture: Werdnerd's miniature pet ram has a lot of energy and is *difficult to control.* Werdnerd's shins are bruised and knotty because he can't keep the ram from bumping his shins. The *ram bumps shins* all the time! Werdnerd's knee-high superhero boots conceal the bruises, but the lumps are visible.

captious: (**kap**-shuhs) **adjective** – making much of trivial faults or defects; difficult to please

synonyms: carping, demanding, disparaging, exacting, nit-picking

origin: From the Latin *captiosus,* meaning "fallacious."

example: I don't know why my **captious** boss doesn't just fire me. To hear him tell it, I can't do anything right.

memory word: cap-shoes

picture: A nun at a Catholic school is very *difficult to please.* She *finds fault* with everything about little Werdnerd, from his *cap* to his *shoes.*

umbrage: (**uhm**-brij) **noun** – offense; annoyance; displeasure

synonyms: huff, indignation, injury, irritation, resentment

origin: From the Latin *umbraticum*, meaning "of or pertaining to shade."

example: The president has really thin skin and takes **umbrage** at the slightest criticism.

memory word: dumb-bridge

picture: As a ship passes through a drawbridge, the bridge comments, "If you keep putting on weight, you might not fit next time." The ship takes *offense* and demonstrates its *indignation* by bumping the bridge several times, bellowing, *"Dumb bridge!"*

narcissistic: (nahr-suh-**sis**-tik) **adjective** – being in love with oneself; overly self-admiring

synonyms: conceited, egotistic, self-centered, stuck-up, vain

origin: In Greek mythology, *Narcissus* was a handsome young man who saw his reflection in a pool of water and fell in love with himself. He could not pull himself away from his visage, so he wasted away. The gods felt sorry for him and turned him into a flower. The narcissus flower, a.k.a. daffodil, is one of the most popular flowers in the world.

example: Those who post duck-face selfies on social media all day long might be a bit **narcissistic**.

memory word: horse-assistant

picture: *Deeply in love with himself,* a beautiful horse has his **horse assistant** follow him everywhere, holding up a full-length mirror so he can admire himself at all times.

pedagogue: (**ped**-uh-gog) **noun** – a strict, dull, and overly formal teacher

synonyms: educator, instructor, lecturer, pedant, professor, schoolmaster

origin: From the Greek *paidagogos*, meaning "slave who escorts boys to school and generally supervises them."

example: The **pedagogue** stood in front of the class in the same spot every day and lectured in a monotone voice while the students struggled to pay attention.

memory word: pet-a-dog

picture: You join a group at the park for some dog training. The *strict, dull, and overly formal instructor* takes all of the fun out of it. She says, "There's my way and the wrong way to handle your dog. Let's start with how to *pet a dog*. Hold your leash exactly like this and . . ."

vituperative: (vayh-**too**-per-uh-tiv) **adjective** – using, containing, or marked by harshly abusive criticism

synonyms: castigating, disparaging, offensive, scathing, vilipendious

origin: From the Latin *vituperare*, meaning "to disparage."

example: A simple reprimand would have been sufficient, but the boss lost his temper and unloaded with a 20-minute **vituperative** rant.

memory word: buy-two-for-a-gift

picture: The sign at the bookstore states, *"Buy two for a gift."* So you bite. You buy two books and receive a gift of a balloon on a string, sending you into an ***abusive and scathing*** rant, "Do I look like a %$#@* child? This is the gift? How would you like it if I took this balloon and shoved it . . . ?"

nugatory: (**noo**-guh-tawr-ee) **adjective** – of no real value; of no force or effect; not valid

synonyms: trifling, useless, worthless; futile, ineffective; null and void

origin: From the Latin *nugari,* meaning "to trifle, jest, play the fool."

example: Politicians do not believe the tripe in their **nugatory** speeches. They pander to their constituents, telling them what they want to hear.

memory word: nougat-only

picture: Werdnerd kicks his feet up and relaxes with a good dictionary. While he reads, he dips his *nougat* bar into some gooey chocolate. He muses, "***Nougat only* is *worthless.*** The chocolate coating is essential."

salubrious: (suh-**loo**-bree-uhs) **adjective** – favorable to or promoting health

synonyms: beneficial, good, healthful, salutary, sanitary, wholesome

origin: From the Latin *salubris*, meaning "promoting health, healthful."

example: The mountain air and coastal environs are both very **salubrious** due to the negative ions generated by the trees and waves.

memory word: saloon-Prius

picture: The *Saloon Prius,* a saloon adjacent to a local coffee shop, features prime parking up front, reserved for the Prius drivers. The saloon serves only organic, ***wholesome, healthy*** drinks to the health-nut Prius drivers.

meander: (mee-**an**-der) **verb** – to wander aimlessly; to follow a winding course

synonyms: ramble, roam, snake, stray, stroll, twist, wind, zigzag

origin: From the Greek *Maiandros*, a river in Turkey famous for its winding course.

example: My history teacher in high school was easily distracted. Almost every day, we got him to **meander** off topic and tell war stories.

memory word: me-and-her

picture: A couple of love birds honeymoon in Rome. They revel in taking long walks, relishing the sights. He texts his parents, *"Me and her wander all over Rome from sunup to sundown!"*

luminary: (**loo**-muh-ner-ee) **noun** – a celestial body, as the sun or moon; a body or object that gives light; a person who has attained eminence in his or her field and/or is an inspiration to others

synonyms: celebrity, dignitary, leader, lion, superstar, VIP

origin: From the Latin *lucere,* meaning "to shine."

example: Rush Limbaugh, Mark Levin, Glenn Beck, and Bill O'Reilly are hated by some, but **luminaries** to others.

memory word: Lou-and-Mary

picture: *Lou and Mary* sell all of their worldly possessions and devote the rest of their lives to visiting orphanages, soup kitchens, and homeless shelters, helping the less fortunate. *Lou and Mary* are *objects of light* who are *an inspiration to others.*

anathema: (uh-**nath**-uh-muh) **noun** – a person or thing detested, loathed, accursed, or consigned to damnation or destruction

synonyms: abomination, bane, curse, enemy, execration, pariah, taboo

origin: This is a loan word (same spelling and meaning) from Greek.

example: Tax increases and more government regulations are **anathemas** to a constitutional conservative.

memory word: an-anthem-ma

picture: A college freshman returns home at Thanksgiving. She's humming a tune, and her mom asks what it is. She responds, "*An anthem, ma*. Commie Tommy taught a communist anthem to a bunch of us." Mom snaps, "Well, Commie Tommy can pay your tuition from now on as I *detest* anything smacking of communism."

bleak: (bleek) **adjective** – desolate and windswept; without hope or encouragement

synonyms: discouraging, dismal, dreary, gloomy, hopeless, unpromising

example: Many people saw a **bleak** future during the Great Depression.

memory word: beak

picture: A couple of vultures perch on the limb of a dead tree in a *desolate*, *windswept* desert, waiting for their next meal. One vulture is all *beak*. The other one asks, "You know there's **no hope** of you getting a date with that beak, don't you?"

replete: (ri-**pleet**) **adjective** – abundantly supplied or provided; filled

synonyms: abounding, awash, brimming, jammed, packed, rife, teeming

origin: From the Latin *replere*, meaning "to fill, fill again."

example: Washington D.C. is **replete** with crooked politicians.

memory word: re-pleat

picture: A school uniform supply store is *abundantly supplied* with pleated skirts. As soon as the cashier sells a pleated skirt, she shouts, "*Re-Pleat*," signaling a stock clerk to replace it with another of the same size and color.

onerous: (oh-ner-uhs) **adjective** – having or involving obligations or responsibilities, especially legal ones that outweigh the advantages

synonyms: arduous, burdensome, grueling, oppressive, ponderous

origin: From the Latin *onerosus*, meaning "burdensome."

example: The 2016 U.S. tax code, unbelievably complex and **onerous,** weighs in at 74,608 pages!

memory word: owner-Russ

picture: A regular at a restaurant asks the waitress, "So, how do you like working for the new owner, Russell?" She says, "OMG! The work is *grueling*, and the ***owner, Russ,*** is so *oppressive.* Believe it or not, he brought in a whip this morning. He cracks it at us as we walk by and yells 'Hustle! Hustle! Hustle!'"

negate: (ni-**gayt**) **verb** – to nullify or cause to be ineffective; to deny or contradict

synonyms: annul, cancel out, invalidate, neutralize, repeal, revoke, void

origin: From the Latin *negare*, meaning "to deny, say no."

example: One weak link in a chain **negates** the strength of all the others.

memory word: neck-ache

picture: Michelangelo is getting a neck massage to *neutralize* the *neck ache* resulting from painting the ceiling of the Sistine Chapel.

paradox: (par-uh-doks) **noun** – a statement that contradicts itself

synonyms: Catch-22, enigma, nonsense, opposite, puzzle, riddle

origin: From the Greek *paradoxos*, meaning "contrary to expectation."

example: Many children enjoy the humorous **paradox** of nonsense verse such as, "Early in the morning, in the middle of night, two dead boys got up to fight. Back to back, they faced each other. They drew their swords and shot each other. A deaf policeman heard the noise. He came and shot the two dead boys. If you don't believe this lie is true, ask the blind man. He saw it too."

memory word: pair-of-ducks

picture: One duck, trying to mess with another duck's mind, quips, "This statement is false." The other duck retorts, "If so, then it is a ***contradiction***. If the statement is true, then it must be false, thereby making it true. However, take everything I say with a grain of salt because I always lie." The first duck says, "Then what you just said must be true and not a lie." The ***pair of ducks*** continues this circle of ***nonsense*** for hours.

winnow: (**win**-oh) **verb** – the act of separating grain from chaff; to blow upon; select desirable parts from a group or list

synonyms: analyze, eliminate, examine, extract, remove, select, sieve, sort

origin: **Winnow** may stem from the Latin *vannus*, meaning "winnowing fan," or it is possible it comes from *ventilare*, meaning "to brandish, toss in the air, fan, agitate."

example: When asked to name his top ten favorite sesquipedalian words, Werdnerd got a gleam in his eye and began mental gymnastics, **winnowing** out those multi-syllabic words that didn't fit on his list.

memory word: minnow

picture: While a little boy fishes with his dad, he gets sidetracked corralling dozens of minnows into a net. Noticing there are a few purple *minnow*s, he carefully *separates* these distinguished little fish from the common ones.

discrepant: (dih-**skrep**-uhnt) **adjective** – not in agreement

synonyms: conflicting, contrary, different, incompatible, incongruent

origin: From the Latin *discrepare*, meaning "to sound discordant."

example: They could not be a more **discrepant** couple. He is tall, thin, content, and taciturn. She is short, plump, peevish, and loquacious.

memory word: this-crap-ain't

picture: A self-described "intellectual" student in college *disagrees* with every student and the professor during class discussions. He takes the *opposite* side of every issue, quite often grunting, *"This crap ain't* convincing me in the least."

badger: (baj-er) **verb** – to harass, annoy, or urge persistently

synonyms: bug, bully, goad, hassle, hound, needle, pester, ride, torment

example: The children **badgered** their parents until they relented and took them to the water park.

memory word: badger

picture: A cete (a group of *badgers*) is *pestering* their mom to let them go out and play in the rain. Mom snaps, "For the 50th time—NO! You'll all catch a cold."

abjure: (ab-**joor**) **verb** – to renounce, repudiate, or retract, especially under oath

synonyms: abstain, forswear, recant, reject, swear off, withdraw

origin: From the Latin *abiurare*, meaning "to deny on oath."

example: I tried sushi once and got food poisoning. I **abjure** sushi.

memory word: ab-juror

picture: A juror in the murder trial of the century is so fat he cannot fit in the assigned seating. The judge tells him he has one week until the trial commences to fit in that seat, insisting, "I want to see **ab**s, *juror!*" The *ab juror renounces* all food and drink except for celery and water for the next week.

adjure: (uh-**joor**) **verb** – to charge, bind, or command earnestly and solemnly, often under oath or the threat of a penalty

synonyms: implore, obligate, order, require, supplicate

origin: From the Latin *adiurare*, meaning "to confirm by oath."

example: "Then some of the itinerant Jewish exorcists undertook to invoke the name of the Lord Jesus over those who had evil spirits, saying, 'I **adjure** you by the Jesus whom Paul proclaims.'" (Acts 19:13)

memory word: add-juror

picture: The trial starts a week later. Sitting next to the ab juror, an *add juror* holds an abacus in her lap and makes a constant racket as she adds this and that. The judge **commands** her to relinquish the abacus to the bailiff.

calumny: (kal-uhm-nee) **noun** – a false and malicious statement designed to injure the reputation of someone or something

synonyms: aspersion, defamation, derogation, libel, lie, slander

origin: From the Latin *calumnia*, meaning "subterfuge, malicious charge." In Roman law, a person who made a false accusation was branded on the forehead with the letter K (the initial of old Latin *kalumniator*, or "slanderer").

example: "A man calumniated is doubly injured. First by him who utters the **calumny**, and then by him who believes it." (Herodotus)

memory word: cow-on-knee

picture: A ventriloquist performs a rather abrasive act. His dummy, a cow, tells coarse jokes, *lies, and slanders* public figures. No one can accuse the ventriloquist of *defamation*, however, since the *cow on* his *knee* is the one casting *aspersions*.

didactic: (dahy-**dak**-tik) **adjective** – intended for instruction; inclined to teach or lecture others too much

synonyms: academic, educational, moralizing, pedantic, sermonizing

origin: From the Greek *didaskein*, meaning "to teach."

example: The intention of the *Visualize Your Vocabulary* series is to be simultaneously **didactic** and entertaining.

memory word: die-bad-tick

picture: A tick *preaches a sermon* to his congregation. He *lectures* and admonishes them to repent and be good ticks, or they will *die bad tick*s and burn in a dog-forsaken hell for eternity.

maudlin: (**mawd**-lin) **adjective** – tearfully or weakly emotional; foolishly sentimental because of drunkenness

synonyms: bathetic, drippy, mushy, sappy, schmaltzy, syrupy, weepy

origin: Maudlin comes from Mary Magdalene, the repentant sinner forgiven by Jesus in Luke 7:37-38. She washed his feet with her tears and is often shown weeping in paintings.

example: The 1994 movie *Forrest Gump* is often amusing. However, the scene where Forrest Gump learns that he has a son and wonders if his boy is slow-witted (like him) is one of the more **maudlin** moments.

memory word: Maude-Lynn

picture: Aunt *Maude Lynn* is *foolishly sentimental*. At family gatherings, she constantly reminisces about deceased family members. She puts one hand on her chest, waves the other one as if to dry her teary eyes, and sobs, "Give me a moment, I'm getting verklempt. Talk amongst yourselves. Don't worry about me."

cogent: (koh-juhnt) **adjective** – powerfully persuasive or convincing

synonyms: compelling, conclusive, influential, pertinent, significant

origin: From the Latin *cogere*, meaning "to drive together; to compel."

example: Senator Simpleton wouldn't know a **cogent** thought if it smacked him on the brain.

memory word: cold-gent

picture: A gentleman stands shivering on a stranger's doorstep. He begs, pleads, and entreats her to let him come in to warm up, as it is freezing outside. Finding his entreaties *powerfully persuasive,* she invites in the *cold gent*.

miscreant: (**mis**-kree-unht) **noun** – an evildoer

synonyms: criminal, hoodlum, malefactor, reprobate, villain

example: Social media attracts too many **miscreants**.

memory word: mystery-ant

picture: A human-sized *reprobate* ant lurks in dark alleys at night. A police sketch depicts him wearing a black hat, a scarf, and a trench coat. His victims have never seen anything but the eyes of the *criminal mystery ant.*

unctuous: (**uhngk**-choo-uhs) **adjective** – unpleasantly suave or ingratiating in manner or speech; oily or greasy

synonyms: groveling, insincere, obsequious, servile, sycophantic

origin: From the Latin *unctus*, meaning "act of anointing with oil."

example: The **unctuous** used-car salesman almost had me convinced that he was my best friend.

memory word: monk-chew-us

picture: While a monk eats a plate of *greasy* fries, one fry says to another, "Well, it was nice knowing you. It's all over when the ***monk chew*s *us.***"

malefactor: (**mal**-uh-fak-ter) **noun** – a person who does harm or evil, especially one who commits a crime

synonyms: delinquent, evildoer, hoodlum, outlaw, thug, villain

origin: From the Latin *malefacere,* meaning "to do evil."

example: My representative is a **malefactor** who engaged in malfeasance and voter fraud to get elected.

memory word: mallet-factory

picture: A man works in a *mallet factory* testing mallets by pounding an iron anvil. If the mallet doesn't break, it passes inspection. He's an *evil person* because he sneaks up on other employees and whacks them on the head with the mallet.

admonish: (ad-**mon**-ish) **verb** – to caution, advise, or counsel against something; to reprove or scold mildly

synonyms: exhort, warn; censure, chide, reprimand

origin: From the Latin *admonere*, meaning "to remind, suggest, advise."

example: A judge always **admonishes** the jury to keep certain things in mind while weighing the evidence and reaching a verdict.

memory word: add-polish

picture: A father says to his son, who washes and waxes his car every day, "I'd *advise* you to ease off and just *add polish* every couple of months. You're going to rub the paint off that car."

egotist: (ee-guh-tist) **noun** – a conceited, boastful, self-centered person

synonyms: boaster, braggart, egoist, egomaniac, narcissist, swellhead

example: The average politician is an **egotist**, cheater, liar, and high tech thief. Did I miss anything?

memory word: Igor-is

picture: Some mad scientists get together after work for a few drinks. One of them asks, "Have you guys noticed the change in Igor? He's turned into a *narcissist*. He can't stop talking about his beautiful bulging eyes and his gorgeous hump. *Igor is* insufferable!"

foil: (foil) **verb** – to prevent the success of; to set off by contrast; **noun** – a person or thing that makes another seem better by contrast

synonyms: block, checkmate, defeat, hinder, prevent, stymie, thwart

example: The Road Runner always manages to **foil** the schemes of Wile E. Coyote.

memory word: foil (tin)

picture: You have watched too many sci-fi movies. You believe that aliens are attempting to hypnotize the human race with radio waves in order to make us passive and slavish before they invade. You line the inside of your house with tin *foil* to *block* this radio frequency.

pare: (pair) **verb** – to cut off the outer coating, layer, or part of

synonyms: carve, crop, flay, prune, scalp, scrape, shave, shear, skin

origin: From the Latin *parare*, meaning "to make ready, furnish, provide."

example: I prefer to eat my veggies and fruit with the peel attached, but my wife, who cooks my meals, insists on **paring** everything.

memory word: pear

picture: A *pear* takes a paring knife and *removes its* own *skin!*

tangent: (**tan**-juhnt) **noun** – a topic nearly or completely unrelated to the main topic; a straight line that touches a curve at a point but does not intersect it at that point

synonyms: aside, departure, digression, discursion, parenthesis

origin: From the Latin *tangere*, meaning "to touch."

example: When Savannah's brain was full, she led her math teacher off on a **tangent** by asking him if he watched the football game last night. Ten minutes later, he returned to the geometry lesson on intersecting **tangent** lines as they relate to curves and spheres.

memory word: tanned-gent

picture: A tanned gentleman professor lectures on the mathematical concept of a tangent. However, he keeps *veering off topic* with comments about his recent ski trip. The *tanned gent* has a skier's raccoon face.

vicarious: (vahy-**kair**-ee-uhs) **adjective** – felt or undergone as if one were taking part in the experience of another; endured or done by a substitute

synonyms: by proxy, delegated, deputed, empathetic, surrogate

origin: From the Latin *vicarius*, meaning "substitute."

example: Studying history is the closest thing to traveling back in time and **vicariously** experiencing events.

memory word: why-carry-us

picture: Two little rich girls dressed up in their moms' clothes are walking along the sidewalk carrying their expensive lap dogs. They are pretending to be like ostentatious Hollywood stars who parade around with their expensive dogs. Meanwhile, the poor little dogs are thinking, "*Why carry us*? We want to walk, too. Ooooh! Check out the fire hydrant!"

stultify: (**stuhl**-tuh-fahy) **verb** – to cause to appear foolish; to deprive of strength; to make useless or worthless

synonyms: make a fool of, mock; cripple, negate, stifle, weaken

origin: From the Latin *stultificare*, meaning "to turn into foolishness."

example: Kryptonite is the only thing that can **stultify** Superman.

memory word: stilt-if-I

picture: Little Werdnerd calls out to the Uncle Sam stilt walker in the Veterans Day parade, "Hey! How's the weather up there?" Uncle Sam jokes, "Real original, kid. I've never heard that one before. Hey, nerd, you should try stilt walking, it's fun." Werdnerd answers, "Naw, I'd try *stilts if I* wasn't afraid of *making a fool of* myself."

excoriate: (ik-**skohr**-ee-ayt) **verb** – to express strong disproval

synonyms: berate, castigate, censure, chastise, reprove, upbraid

origin: From the Latin *excoriare*, meaning "to flay, strip off the hide."

example: The Humane Letters teacher **excoriated** Werdnerd when he corrected her pronunciation of "indefatigable."

memory word: X-Cory-ate

picture: Cory has eaten most of the Scrabble pieces. This time, Mom *expresses strong disapproval* concerning the ***X Cory ate.*** She growls, "There's only one X, Cory, and you ate it."

ordeal: (awr-**deel**) **noun** – a severe or trying experience

synonyms: anguish, crucible, difficulty, test, torment, trial

example: Savannah's junior year of Physics was an **ordeal**.

memory word: or-deal

picture: Would you rather spend a day with your mother-in-law *or deal* with a car salesman, haggling over the price all day? Most people consider them equally *trying experiences.*

bombard: (bom-**bahrd**) **verb** – to attack with literal or figurative artillery fire

synonyms: barrage, beset, besiege, blitz, harass, hound, pester, pound

example: Werdnerd didn't stand a chance when all of his classmates **bombarded** him with spit-wads.

memory word: bomb-bard

picture: An audience *hurls bombs* at Shakespeare (a.k.a. "the bard"). They *bomb bard* relentlessly.

idealist: (ahy-**dee**-uh-list) **noun** – a person who cherishes or pursues high or noble principles, purposes, goals, etc.; a visionary or impractical person

synonyms: dreamer, optimist, Platonist, romantic, utopian

origin: From the Latin *idealis*, meaning "existing in idea."

example: The few good politicians go to D.C. as **idealists,** thinking they can change things, but end up as demoralized cogs in the machinery.

memory word: idea-list

picture: A little girl overhears her parents fretting over the heat wave and the high electric bill. The little *optimist* presents them with an *idea list*. Idea number one—move to the North Pole for the summer and spend some quality time with Santa. Idea number two—put a snow-making machine on the roof.

manifold: (**man**-uh-fohld) **adjective** – of many kinds; numerous and varied

synonyms: copious, diverse, multifold, multitudinous, sundry, various

example: The class nerd always puts her inimitable spin on things. Instead of saying, "There's more than one way to skin a cat" she says, "There are **manifold** ways of skinning a feline."

memory word: man-I-fold

picture: You create one origami design after another. Your friend asks when you learned this amazing art. You reply, "I didn't. I woke up from a coma after being struck by lightning and the next thing I knew, I was an expert origamist. ***Man, I fold numerous*** new designs every day."

atone: (uh-**tohn**) **verb** – to make amends or reparation for an offense, crime, or sin

synonyms: absolve, do penance, expiate, recompense, redeem, square

origin: *Atone* is a contraction of "at" and "one." It is believed to stem from the Latin *adunare*, meaning "to unite."

example: Some who believe in man-made "global warming" go so far as to buy "carbon offsets" to **atone** for their perceived personal contribution to polluting the air.

memory word: a-tone

picture: Confessions are down. People aren't *repenting* like they used to. So, the priest rigs up a button on the podium which he pushes upon finishing a sermon. *A tone* rings throughout the church, hypnotizing the parishioners and compelling them to line up at the confession booth.

libel: (lahy-buhl) **noun** – defamation by written or printed words, pictures or any form other than by spoken words

synonyms: aspersion, calumny, defamation, denigration, smear

origin: From the Latin *libellus*, meaning "a little book, pamphlet, petition, written accusation, complaint." It is a diminutive of *liber*, meaning "book."

example: Many people confuse **libel** and slander. These words have similar meanings, but slander is spoken, not written. If you can remember that **libel** stems from the Latin word that means "book," you will be able to distinguish **libel** from slander.

memory word: lie-bull

picture: Farmer John catches his bull early one morning writing a bunch of *damaging statements* on the side of his red barn. He confronts him: "You *lie, bull!* Yer not gonna get away with this *defamation*. I'm gonna fetch some paint and yer gonna fix yer mess, or I'll commence to castrat'n ya."

repertoire: (**rep**-er-twahr) **noun** – the entire range of skills, techniques, devices, or aptitudes used in a particular occupation or field; a collection of works an actor or singer can perform

synonyms: repository, stockpile, store, supply

origin: From the Latin *repertorium*, meaning "an inventory."

example: The lunch lady at McCamey High School has an endless **repertoire** of recipes. The students never have the same meal twice.

memory word: the-parrot-war

picture: Two parrots engage in a presidential debate, in which each uses its *entire range of skills and lexicon.* This epic verbal dual goes down in history as *The Parrot War* of Ideas.

vintage: (**vin**-tij) **noun** – the specific year a wine was made; **adjective** – representing the high quality of times past; old-fashioned

synonyms: crop, harvest; choice, classic, excellent, rare, select, venerable

example: Werdnerd cares not a whit for a bottle of **vintage** 1967 wine, but he would like a **vintage** 1967 Mustang.

memory word: bandage

picture: A *classic* car, a *choice* bottle of wine, and a *rare* movie reel of *Gone with the Wind* have all been *bandage*d.

Visualize Your Vocabulary   75

taper: (**tay**-per) **verb** – to diminish gradually; to become smaller or thinner on one end

synonyms: dwindle, fade, lessen, recede, subside, wane, wind down

example: Veteran marathoners **taper** their training a week or two before an event.

memory word: tapeworm

picture: While jogging, one *tapeworm* says to another, "My running coach has been *gradually reducing* my miles the last few days. She says it's the best way to hit peak performance without overtraining."

objective: (uhb-**jek**-tiv) **adjective** – not influenced by emotion or personal bias; based on observable phenomena

synonyms: impartial, impersonal, open-minded, unbiased; quantitative

origin: From the Latin *obiectum*, meaning "impersonal, unbiased."

example: News reporters are incapable of delivering an **objective** account of a story; they can't refrain from injecting their bias.

memory word: object-give

picture: Dr. Frankenstein creates a companion for his first hulking creation. The mad scientist presents "the bride of Frankenstein" and asks the grotesque hulk, "Well? How do you like her?" Frankenstein shrugs *emotionless*ly, hands her the rose from his lapel, and grunts, "Me *object give* you."

subjective: (suhb-**jek**-tiv) **adjective** – influenced by personal feelings, intuitions, tastes, or opinions

synonyms: biased, personal, prejudiced, qualitative

origin: From the Latin *subiectivus*, meaning "of the subject."

example: Werdnerd thinks he is a brilliant walking and talking dictionary. However, his high opinion of himself is **subjective**; his mom is the only one who shares his elevated notion of himself.

memory word: sub-jet-tiff

picture: A submarine and a jet engage in a heated conversation that exposes their *biases and prejudices.* Finally giving up trying to convince each other of their *opinions,* they stomp off in a huff in opposite directions. Several onlookers witness this *sub jet tiff.*

balm: (bahm) **noun** – an aromatic semi-solid substance used to heal and soothe; a plant yielding such compound; a fragrant or sweet aroma

synonyms: analgesic, balsam, emollient, ointment, poultice, salve

example: Mia has an assortment of fragrant lip **balms**.

memory word: palm

picture: A *palm* tree leans over to rub a *soothing, fragrant ointment* on the sore spot where someone cut it with an ax.

demean: (dih-**meen**) **verb** – to lower in dignity, honor, or worth

synonyms: belittle, debase, derogate, disparage, put down, stoop

origin: From the Latin *minari*, meaning "to use threats."

example: The senator **demeaned** himself by accepting bribes.

memory word: D-mean

picture: The letters of the alphabet stand on a ladder in ascending order. The D reaches up and grabs the E and pulls it off, telling it to *lick the floor and stay where it belongs*. The *D mean.*

piquant: (pee-kahnt) **adjective** – having an agreeably pungent or sharp taste; engagingly stimulating or provocative

synonyms: savory, spicy, tangy, zesty; interesting, lively, spirited

example: Just looking at the **piquant** items on the menu made my mouth water and my taste buds dance with anticipation.

memory word: pecan

picture: A *pecan*'s lips pucker and its face contorts as it savors the *pungent flavor* of its favorite candy . . . Sweetarts.

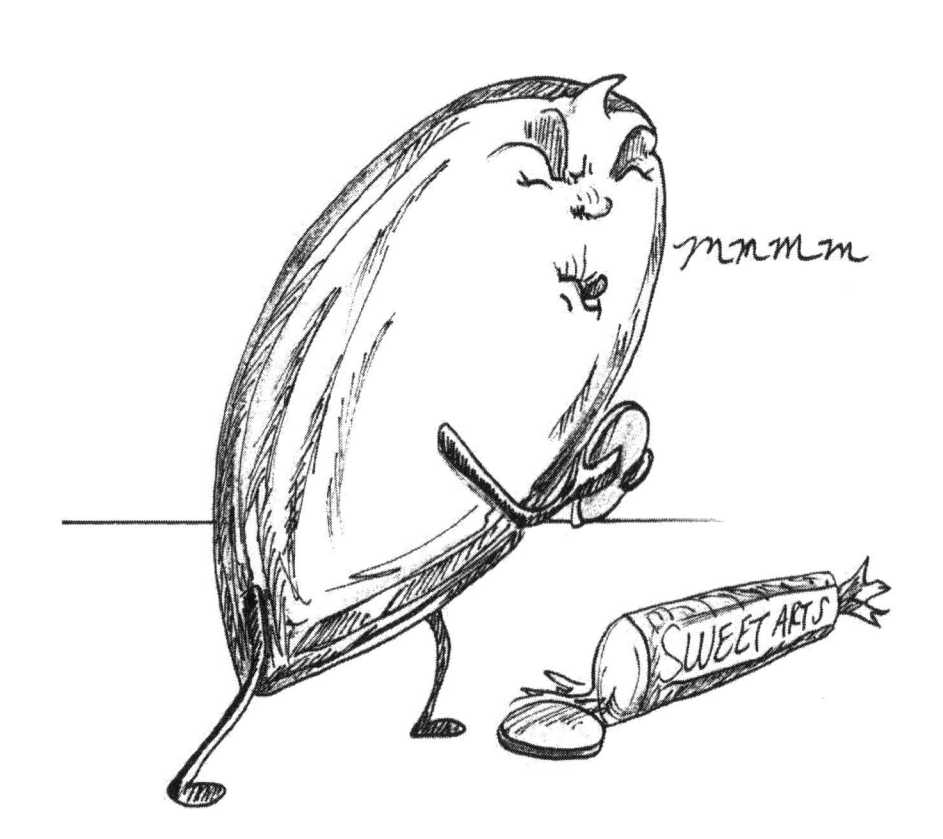

arrogate: (**ar**-uh-gayt) **verb** – to seize and take control presumptuously and without authority

synonyms: appropriate, commandeer, confiscate, expropriate, usurp

origin: From the Latin *arrogare*, meaning "to claim for oneself."

example: Billy the bully shoved Werdnerd to the ground and **arrogated** his thesaurus.

memory word: arrow-gate

picture: A band of marauding Vikings raids your neighborhood. One Viking shoots arrows at whatever he wants *to claim as his own.* After his arrow pierces your front gate, he proclaims, "This *arrow gate* and everything within its boundaries are mine!"

procure: (proh-**kyoor**) **verb** – to acquire or bring about by care, effort, or the use of special means

synonyms: engineer, land, obtain, score, wrangle

origin: From the Latin *procurare*, meaning "to take care of."

example: To arrogate is illegal and heavy handed; to **procure** is legal and requires finesse.

memory word: broke-your

picture: Werdnerd returns the vintage golf clubs you loaned him. He says, "I *broke your* favorite putter. You wouldn't believe what I went through to *obtain* one exactly like it. The guy I *acquired* it from in Scotland claims only two of them exist, and he sold his to me!"

bearing: (**bair**-ing) **noun** – the characteristic way in which one conducts or carries oneself

synonyms: behavior, comportment, demeanor, manner, poise, presence

example: Mr. Giles French has the quintessential **bearing** of a butler.

memory word: bear-ring

picture: A bear exits a pawn shop wearing a Super Bowl ring. Wearing the *bear ring* engenders a drastic change in his *demeanor*. He struts down the sidewalk bragging, "That's right. We bad!"

oust: (oust) **verb** – to expel or remove from an office or position

synonyms: depose, dethrone, displace, eject, fire, relegate, unseat

origin: From the Latin *obstare*, meaning "to stand opposite to."

example: After Werdnerd *ousted* the reigning spelling bee champion, he did a goofy celebratory dance, pretending to spike the trophy as if it were a football.

memory word: house

picture: Because one dilapidated *house* in a gated community breaks all of the Home Owners Association's rules and regulations, the other houses *force it out* of the neighborhood.

qualitative: (kwol-i-tay-tiv) **adjective** – pertaining to or concerned with distinctions based on quality or qualities

synonyms: conditional, dependent, subjective

origin: From the Latin *qualitativus*, meaning "relating to quality."

example: Werdnerd would rather have one high-quality skinsuit and a cape than a dozen shoddy ones. He is more concerned with the **qualitative** aspect of his attire than the quantitative.

memory word: koala-tater

picture: A panel of koalas samples a variety of potatoes to determine their *quality*. The *koala tater* panel rarely agrees because the members' tastes vary.

somatic: (soh-**mat**-ik) **adjective** – pertaining to the body as opposed to the mind or spirit

synonyms: carnal, corporal, fleshly, physical, sensual, tangible

origin: From the Greek *somatikos*, meaning "of the body."

example: After a battery of tests, Dr. House determined Baron's **somatic** symptoms are a result of Munchausen syndrome, a psychiatric disorder.

memory word: so-mad-at

picture: A headless female *body* says to a headless male *body*, "I'm *so mad at* you. All you care about is my *body*." He responds, "Uh . . . Yeah."

habituate: (huh-**bich**-oo-ayt) **verb** – to make psychologically or physically accustomed to something

synonyms: acclimate, condition, harden, inure, season, train

origin: From the Latin *habituare*, meaning "to bring into a condition or habit."

example: The USMC **habituates** enlisted Marines to perform in any and all situations.

memory word: habit-you-ate

picture: Do you remember the first *habit* (nun's outfit) *you ate?* It was hard to choke down, but now you are *accustomed to* it and eat one every week.

lavish: (**lav**-ish) **adjective** – characterized by extravagance and profusion; **verb** – to expend or give in great amounts

synonyms: bountiful, copious, excessive, opulent; heap, pour, shower

origin: From the Latin *lavare*, meaning "to wash, bathe, soak."

example: Senator McLame lives a **lavish** lifestyle in D.C. He only returns to his home state when he seeks re-election.

memory word: lab-dish

picture: As students file into the science lab, the teacher instructs them to carefully select a *lab dish* (petri dish) from the table at the front of the room. Inevitably, a *profusion* of hundreds of *lab dish*es stacked to the ceiling comes crashing down.

renown: (ri-**noun**) **noun** – widespread and high acclaim

synonyms: celebrity, fame, glory, honor, notoriety, repute

example: Werdnerd achieved **renown** upon entrance into the Guinness Book of World Records for the most extensive command of English vocabulary.

memory word: rain-down

picture: Werdnerd is so *highly esteemed and famous* that everywhere he goes confetti *rains down* on him.

pragmatic: (prag-**mat**-ik) **adjective** – having a practical point of view

synonyms: commonsensical, down-to-earth, logical, realistic

origin: From the Greek *pragmatikos*, meaning "business-like, systematic."

example: Expecting unicorns and fairies at your birthday party is not very **pragmatic**, especially if you are turning 18.

memory word: back-matted

picture: Harry, a man with a hairy back, seeks help from a dermatologist.

Doctor: "I've never seen a *back matted* up into dreads."

Harry: "My wife is tired of shaving it, and I'm allergic to the hair removal products. Isn't there a *practical* solution?"

Doctor: "The only *realistic* solution is electrolysis. It's a treatment that destroys the hair follicle so it can't grow hair."

pellucid: (puh-**loo**-sid) **adjective** – allowing the maximum transmission of light; easily understandable

synonyms: limpid, translucent, transparent; comprehensible, simple

origin: From the Latin *pellucidus*, meaning "transparent."

example: Professor Werdnerd seldom delivers **pellucid** lectures because he likes to show off by using grandiloquent words.

memory word: pillow-Sid

picture: A woman asks her husband, Sidney, "Have you seen the ***translucent pillow, Sid?***" He quips, "Well, either Phido is levitating, or he's lying on it."

impecunious: (im-pi-**kyoo**-nee-uhs) **adjective** – having little or no money

synonyms: beggared, broke, destitute, impoverished, indigent

origin: From the Latin *in*, meaning "not" and *pecuniousus*, meaning "rich."

example: After striking oil, the Clampett family went from **impecunious** Ozark country folk to wealthy denizens of Beverly Hills, California.

memory word: them-petunias

picture: A hillbilly sees some petunias holding a sign, begging for money. He says to his kids, "*Them petunias* is worse off than we is."

nocturnal: (nok-**tur**-nl) **adjective** – occurring in, or relating to the night

synonyms: after dark, late, nightly, nighttime

origin: From the Latin *nocturnus*, meaning "belonging to the night."

example: Owls, bats, raccoons, and vampires are **nocturnal**.

memory word: knock-turtle

picture: A turtle sleeps during the day and roams around the neighborhood at *night*. Lonely, he wanders from house to house, knocking on doors. Someone needs to tell the *knock turtle* to go downtown to the *nightclub* where the *night* owls hang out.

filibuster: (fil-uh-buhs-ter) **noun** – a long speech used as a delaying tactic to obstruct legislation; **verb** – to obstruct legislation by talking at great length

synonyms: delay, interference, stonewalling, talkathon

example: South Carolina Senator Strom Thurmond holds the record for the longest **filibuster**. He spoke for over 24 hours.

memory word: Phil-and-Buster

picture: Senators **Phil and Buster** are at it again. Together, they can speak for days to stop a proposed bill from passing.

infallible: (in-**fal**-uh-buhl) **adjective** – incapable of making a mistake; absolutely trustworthy or sure

synonyms: faultless, foolproof, inerrable, perfect, reliable, unfailing

example: Werdnerd thinks he is **infallible,** but he is mistaken.

memory word: in-fowl-and-bull

picture: A global company has thousands of employees who sit at computers entering data all day. The company wants to cut costs and reduce input error, so it replaces all of the employees with chickens and bulls that have computer chips inserted into their brains, rendering them *incapable of making a mistake.* When a reporter asks why they installed the chips *in fowl and bull* instead of in the employees, the CEO says, "The FDA wouldn't approve human trials, and besides, we couldn't pay them in chicken feed and hay."

vagrant: (**vay**-gruhnt) **noun** – a person who wanders about idly and has no permanent home or employment

synonyms: bum, drifter, floater, itinerant, transient, vagabond, wanderer

origin: From the Latin *vagare*, meaning "to wander."

example: The hypocritical politician ended his campaign speech with a bold promise that he would "compassionately end the homeless problem once and for all." A minute later, as he headed for his limo, he shoved a bum, growling, "Out of my way, you filthy **vagrant**!"

memory word: vague-rant

picture: A *homeless person* under an overpass is ranting about something to himself. It's impossible to understand him. You hear mostly gibberish, but can make out "government," "tin foil hat," "Area 51," and "Big Brother is watching." It's a ***vague rant.***

prerogative: (pri-**rog**-uh-tiv) **noun** – an exclusive right, privilege, or power exercised by a person or group of people

synonyms: birthright, claim, exemption, immunity, perquisite, title

origin: From the Latin *prerogativa*, meaning "special right."

example: If entertainment stars want to name their children Moon Unit, Kal-El, or Sage Moonblood, it is their **prerogative.**

memory word: pretty-rock-I-give

picture: The caveman election results are in. One caveman presents a stone to another caveman, grunting, "With this *pretty rock I give* you the power of the presidency and all the *privileges and power* that come with it."

existential: (eg-zi-**sten**-shuhl, ek-si) **adjective** – relating to or dealing with existence

synonyms: experiential, observational, pragmatic, subjective

origin: From the Latin *existentialis*, meaning "pertaining to existence."

example: Beware of adopting the philosophical doctrine of existentialism. Many **existential** teachings, such as those of Sartre and Nietzsche, reject the existence of God.

memory word: egg's-a-stench-shell

picture: A stinky chick breaks out of its rotten shell, proclaiming, "I stink. Therefore, *I am.*" Holding its nose, it exclaims, "Whew! That *egg's a stench shell.* Now, where was I? Oh, yes. To be or not to be . . ."

perplex: (per-**pleks**) **verb** – to cause to be puzzled or bewildered

synonyms: baffle, befuddle, confound, dumbfound, mystify, nonplus

origin: From the Latin *perplexus*, meaning "involved, confused."

example: Werdnerd's classmates are perpetually **perplexed** by his extensive vocabulary.

memory word: purple-X

picture: Standing in the driveway on a school morning, Werdnerd is *bewildered* and scratches his head. A giant *purple X* marks the spot where he parked his car the night before.

eradicate: (ih-**rad**-i-kayt) **verb** – to remove or destroy utterly; to pull up by the roots

synonyms: annihilate, demolish, eliminate, exterminate, obliterate, raze

origin: From the Latin *eradicare,* meaning "to root out."

example: As much as we would like to **eradicate** hunger and poverty, it is impossible. In John 12:8, Jesus says, "You will always have the poor among you, but you will not always have me."

memory word: a-rat-I-hate

picture: A colossal rat the size of a dinosaur stomps down Main Street, *destroying and obliterating* everything in its path. The owner of a brand new car peers out the window of the coffee shop at his crushed car and snaps, "Now, that's *a rat I hate.*"

ossify: (**os**-uh-fahy) **verb** – to convert into or cause to harden like a bone; to become rigid or inflexible in habits, attitudes, or opinions

synonyms: fossilize, petrify, solidify, stiffen

origin: From the Latin *ossis*, meaning "bone."

example: Politicians proclaim, "If elected, I will do the will of the people." However, their political beliefs have long since **ossified,** and after they are elected, they don't listen to the people.

memory word: Oz-if-I

picture: The Tin Man pleads with the rest of *The Wizard of Oz* gang, "Let's hurry! I'll get a heart from *Oz if I* can reach him before my joints seize up and *harden like a bone.*

abduction: (ab-**duhk**-shuhn) **noun** – the illegal act of capturing and carrying away by force; the movement of an arm or leg away from the midline of the body

synonyms: kidnapping, nabbing, seizure, snatching, taking captive

origin: From the Latin *abducere*, meaning "to lead away, take away."

example: Although slavery ended in the United States over a century ago, **abduction** and slavery is thriving in Islamic countries.

memory word: ab-duck-shun

picture: A group of ducks with beer bellies is sitting at the bar in their local pub. A duck with ripped abs joins them, but before he can order a drink, the lady ducks flock around him. This doesn't last long, because the beer belly ducks ***carry him away against his will*** and toss him in the gutter. After the ***ab duck shun,*** they get back to their beers.

buttress: (**buh**-tris) **verb** – to support or prop up; to give encouragement or support

synonyms: assist, boost, brace, reinforce, shore up, strengthen, sustain

example: A good debater **buttresses** his argument with unassailable facts.

memory word: bud-dress

picture: A depressed man's friend always tries to buck him up and *encourage* him. He says to his gloomy friend, "C'mon ***bud, dress*** up and let's go out and paint the town red. We'll have a great time."

sybaritic: (sib-uh-**rit**-ik) **adjective** – characterized by or loving luxury or sensuous pleasure; characteristic of a Sybarite

synonyms: epicurean, hedonistic, indulgent, voluptuary

origin: Sybaris was an ancient Greek city located at the bottom of the boot of Italy. The Sybarites were famous for their hedonism. Thus, *sybaritic* has become a byword for opulent luxury and excessive pleasure seeking.

example: Las Vegas's advertising slogan "What happens here, stays here" hints at the **sybaritic** pleasures the city has to offer tourists.

memory word: sip-or-eat-it

picture: A couple *wallows in luxury.* They surround themselves with pearls, gold coins, diamonds, sensuous food, and drink. Their motto is, "If we can't wear it, smell it, *sip or eat it,* we don't want it."

erstwhile: (**urst**-wahyl) **adjective** – former; of times past

synonyms: bygone, gone by, of yore, olden, old-time, once, past

example: Social media has made it easier for **erstwhile** school friends to connect and stay in touch.

memory word: thirst-wild

picture: Remember *times past,* when things weren't so complicated? You would buy a 16-ounce soda in a convenience store, as it was the only size they offered. Well, now the latest in the "bigger is better" war is a five gallon (640 oz.) container. It has a retractable handle, wheels, and a built-in nuclear cooling system that lasts for 1,000 refills. They call it *ThirstWild*. Low-interest financing is available.

apposite: (**ap**-uh-zit, uh-**poz**-it) **adjective** – fitting and relevant; well-adapted

synonyms: appropriate, apropos, apt, germane, pertinent, suitable, timely

origin: From the Latin *appositus*, meaning "contiguous; fit, suitable."

example: Mom has an **apposite** quote or maxim for every occasion.

memory word: apple-zit

picture: A teenage tech geek lives and breathes Apple products. He spends his time trying to find bugs in software for the iPhone, iPad, and Mac computers. He's so obsessed with Apple that even his zits look like little apples. How *appropriate* that this techie has *apple zits*.

diverse: (dih-**vurs**, **dahy**-vurs) **adjective** – of a different kind, form, character, etc.

synonyms: assorted, disparate, dissimilar, mixed bag, sundry, varied

origin: From the Latin *diversus*, meaning "turned different ways."

example: The United Nations is a **diverse** group of people representing virtually every country in the world.

memory word: divers

picture: A pair of Olympic synchronized *divers* couldn't be more *different*. One is tall, skinny, and hairless. The other is short, tubby, and hairy.

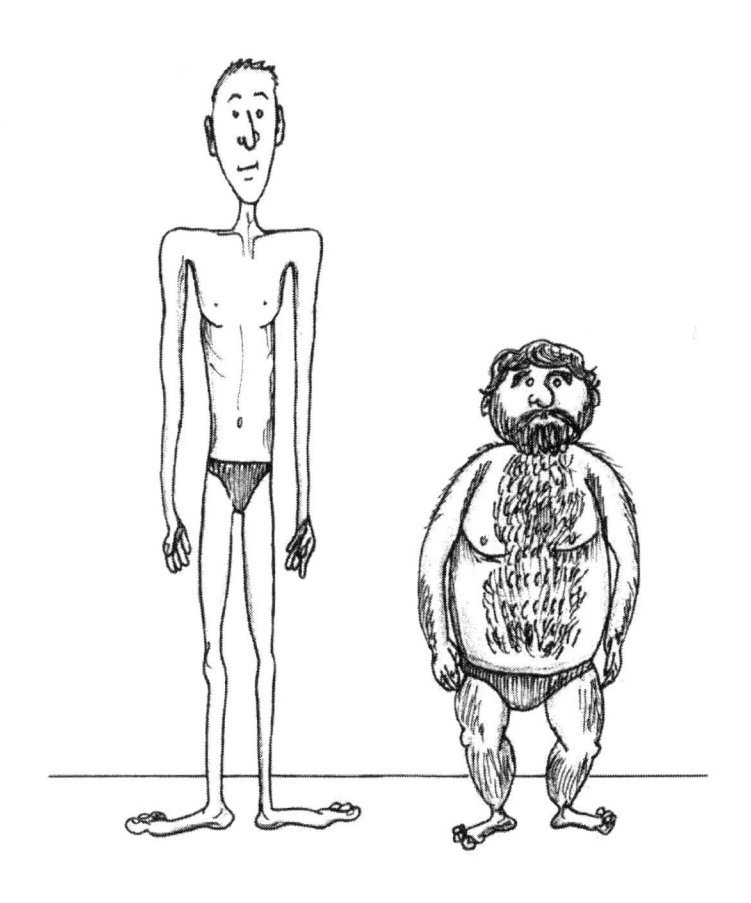

meager: (**mee**-ger) **adjective** – deficient in quantity, quality, fullness, or richness

synonyms: bare, insufficient, little, mere, paltry, scant, small, weak

origin: From the Latin *macer*, meaning "lean, thin."

example: Mom always had a way of putting things into perspective. If I ate only a **meager** portion of my veggies, I got an equally **meager** portion of dessert.

memory word: me-girl

picture: A guy goes on a blind date with a girl who has a very *small* vocabulary. After he introduces himself, she says, "*Me girl*." He mutters to himself, "Oh boy. This is going to be a looooong night."

query: (**kweer**-ee) **noun** – a question; an inquiry; **verb** – to ask or inquire

synonyms: interrogatory; interrogate, investigate, probe, quiz, request

origin: From the Latin *quaerere*, meaning "to seek, look for; to ask."

example: When I send an email **query** to my representative or senators, all I get is an automated response.

memory word: queer-E

picture: Some E's are hangin' out. An odd polka-dotted E with a tail is wearing a feathered cap. One of the other E's wonders, "I just have *to ask*. What's with the *queer E?*"

impromptu: (im-**promp**-too) **adjective** – made or done without previous preparation; suddenly or hastily prepared

synonyms: ad-lib, extemporaneous, improvised, off the cuff, unscripted

origin: From the Latin *in prompt,* meaning "in readiness."

example: The senator relies heavily on his teleprompters when he speaks. Every time he gives an **impromptu** response he embarrasses himself.

memory word: in-prom-too

picture: Awkward and nerdy, young Cicero (perhaps the greatest orator of ancient Rome) decides at the last minute that he wants to attend the prom. The prom chaperone guarding the entrance tells Cicero he can get *in prom too* – but only if he gives a brilliant *off the cuff* speech convincing her why she should allow him in.

embellish: (em-**bel**-ish) **verb** – to make more beautiful by ornamentation; to enhance a statement or narrative with fictitious additions

synonyms: adorn, bedeck, dress up, festoon, garnish, gild; exaggerate

example: Authors Mark Twain and J. Frank Dobie loved to **embellish** their stories with tall tales.

memory word: M-bell-is

picture: A big M is *adorned* with hundreds of colorful bells. The *M bell is* more beautiful *bedecked* this way, though very loud.

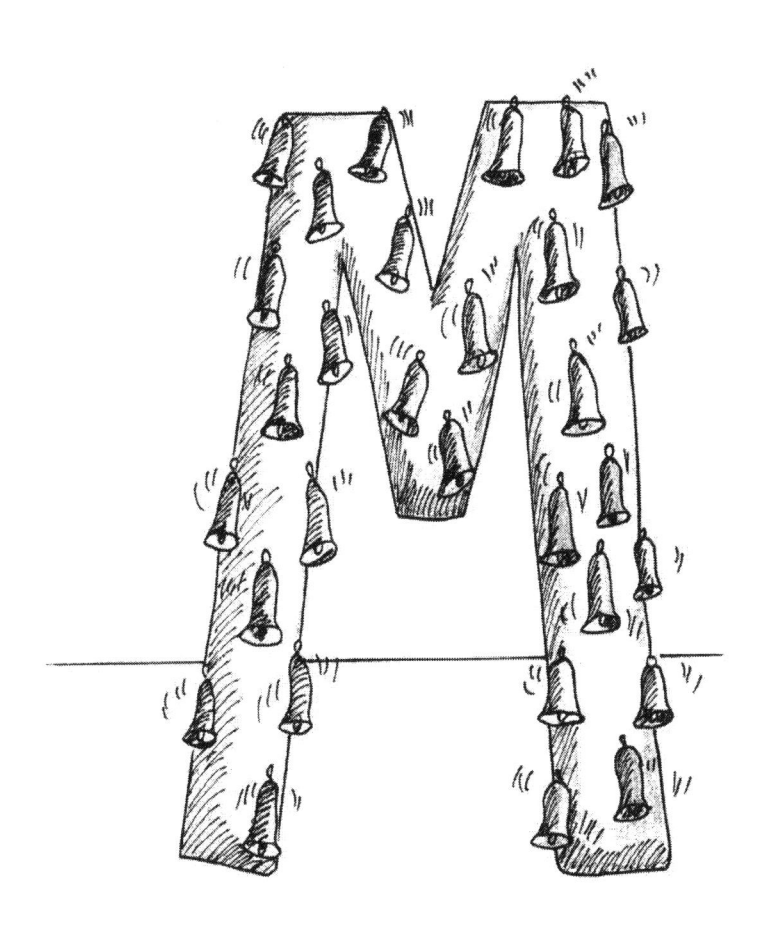

platitude: (**plat**-i-tood) **noun** – a flat, dull, or trite remark, especially one uttered as if it were fresh or profound

synonyms: banality, bromide, cliché, shibboleth

example: My wife and I love bantering back and forth with **platitudes**. What can I say? Birds of a feather flock together.

memory word: plaid-dude

picture: A certain man wears only plaid clothes. He constantly utters Irish *proverbs*, such as, "Here's to our wives and girlfriends; may they never meet"; "The Irish don't know what they want and are prepared to fight to the death to get it"; and "It is often that a person's mouth broke his nose." The *plaid dude* can go on like this all day.

legitimate: (li-jit-uh-mit) **adjective** – according to law; in accordance with established rules, principles, or standards; born in wedlock

synonyms: authorized, lawful, official, recognized, rightful, sanctioned

origin: From the Latin *legitimare,* meaning "to make lawful."

example: Some question the politician's citizenship and don't think he **legitimately** holds the office.

memory word: legit-mutt

picture: Your prize-winning, purebred Alaskan Malamute has a litter of pups. One of them looks like a common mutt. When a potential buyer asks how the ugly one got in the mix, you assure them it is a ***legit mutt,*** and you show them the *official* papers to prove it.

criteria: (krahy-**teer**-ee-uh) **noun** – requirements or standards used to make a decision, judgment, conclusion, or evaluation

synonyms: benchmark, model, norm, rule, scale, touchstone, yardstick

origin: From the Greek *criterion*, meaning "means for judging, standard."

example: Criteria is the plural of *criterion*. The singular form is rarely used because we usually apply more than one standard to render a judgment or conclusion.

memory word: cry-teary-eye

picture: At a crocodile finishing school, one of the *requirements* for graduation is that they must *cry teary eyes* on command. They don't graduate until they can produce perfect crocodile tears (fake sympathy).

transpire: (tran-**spahyr**) **verb** – come about, happen, or occur; to emit or give off waste matter, water vapor, etc., through the surface, as of the body or of leaves

synonyms: arise, befall, come about, develop, ensue, eventuate, gel

example: News junkies cannot wait to see what in the world will **transpire** next.

memory word: trains-pyre

picture: An old timey train stops in the middle of a wooden bridge. Without warning, the bridge catches fire and quickly turns into the *train's pyre* (a pile of wood used for cremating). Now how did that *happen?*

misconstrue: (mis-kuhn-**stroo**) **verb** – to misunderstand the meaning

synonyms: misinterpret, misjudge, misread, mistake, take the wrong way

example: Politicians purposely **misconstrue** the statements of their opponents in order to demonize them.

memory word: Mrs.-Kahn's-stew

picture: Genghis Khan has been out marauding and slaughtering neighboring clans again. He sends a message to Mrs. Khan to be prepared when he gets home to go out dancing and partying. Obviously, she *misunderstood* the message, because when Genghis gets home, she has a Peter Pan costume laid out on the bed and a pot of bean stew on the stove. He says, "What's the meaning of this pansy suit and the famous ***Mrs. Khan's stew?*** I sent a message that I wanted to go dancing and partying." She chortles, "Oh! I thought it was odd that you wanted to go 'prancing and farting'!"

optimist: (**op**-tuh-mist) **noun** – a person disposed to take a favorable view of things

synonyms: dreamer, hoper, idealist, Pollyanna, positivist

origin: From the Latin *optimus*, meaning "the best."

example: A pessimist sees the difficulty in every opportunity; an **optimist** sees the opportunity in every difficulty.

memory word: copter-missed

picture: Your neighbor is always *positive* and happy no matter what happens. So, when a helicopter crashes into his house and bounces off the roof onto his new car, crushing it, you shriek, "Dude! That copter just destroyed everything you own!" He says, "Indeedily doodily, but the way I see it . . . the *copter missed.* Not a scratch on me!"

archaic: (ahr-**kay**-ik) **adjective** – marked by the characteristics of an earlier period

synonyms: ancient, antiquated, antique, old-fashioned, primitive

origin: From the Greek *arkhaios*, meaning "ancient."

example: With the communications technology we have today, it is hard to imagine the **archaic** methods of yore, like smoke signals and the Pony Express.

memory word: arcade

picture: A couple of teens venture into an *arcade* that only has video games from the 70s and 80s, such as Pong, Space Invaders, Donkey Kong, Pac-Man, Frogger, Galaga, Galaxian, and many others. Only their *antiquated* fathers would enjoy those games. What most amazes them is . . . they still work!

slander: (**slan**-der) **noun** – malicious and false spoken words that damage the reputation of another

synonyms: aspersion, calumny, defamation, disparagement, smear

origin: From the Latin *scandalum*, meaning "cause of offense."

example: The politician wrote an op-ed piece in *The New York Times* defaming his opponent. The next day he defamed her while speaking at a press conference. The first day he committed libel; the next day he engaged in **slander**.

memory word: slammed-her

picture: You and your friends are telling "Yo mama" jokes. Someone says to you, "Yo mama is so hairy that Bigfoot wants to take her picture, and yo mama is so ugly that when she went to a beautician, it took 12 hours . . . just to get a quote!" After the laughter dies down, one of your friends says, "Dude, he just *slammed her* so hard. You gotta come back at that *malice*."

imminent: (im-uh-nuhnt) **adjective** – likely to occur at any moment

synonyms: brewing, immediate, impending, inevitable, looming

origin: From the Latin *imminere*, meaning "to overhang; to impend, be near."

example: Animals have a sixth sense, which alerts them to **imminent** danger.

memory word: in-a-minute

picture: A dyslexic doomsdayer holds a sign warning that the end is near. Although he meant to write, "The World's End Is Imminent," he wrote, "The World Ends *in a Minute*."

nuisance: (**noo**-suhns) **noun** – an obnoxious or annoying person, thing, condition, practice, etc.

synonyms: bother, gadfly, headache, irritant, louse, pain, pest, vexation

origin: From the Latin *nocere*, meaning "to hurt."

example: Ethics, morals, and decency are major **nuisances** to politicians.

memory word: noose-ants

picture: A little boy busily makes tiny nooses to hang ants. Trying to get the nooses around the little buggers' necks turns out to be an *irritating* exercise in futility. *Annoyed*, he abandons the *noose ants* project and spends the next several hours burning the ants one by one with his magnifying glass.

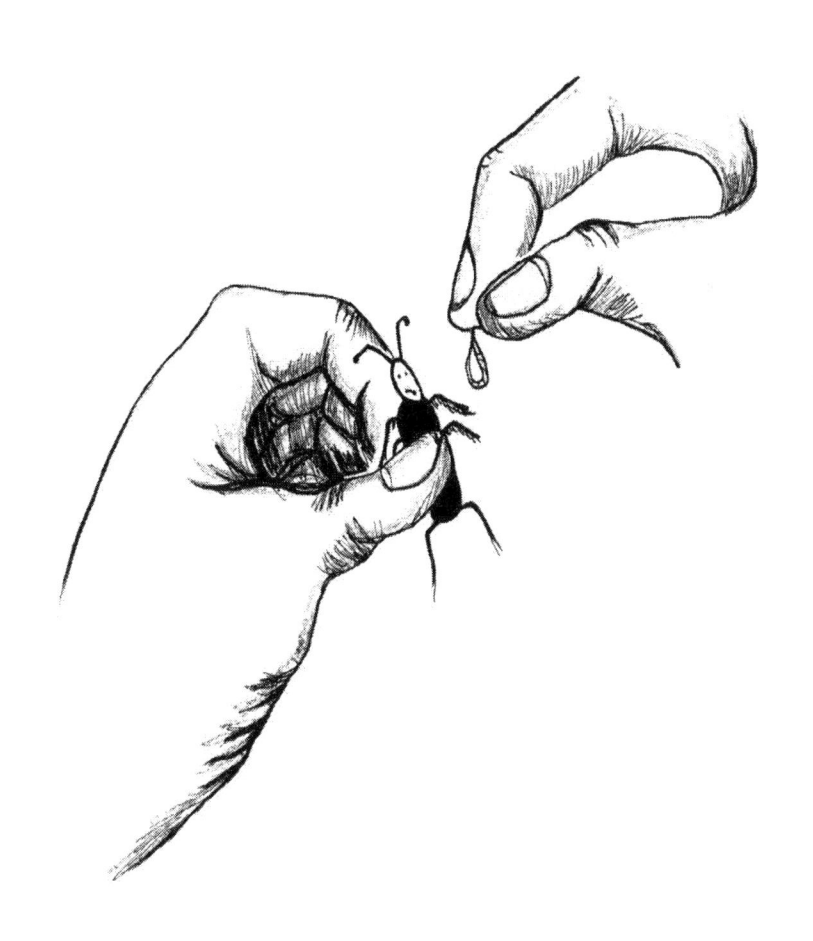

retrospective: (re-truh-**spek**-tiv) **adjective** – looking or directed to the past

synonyms: contemplative, ex post facto, pensive, reflective, retro

example: Grandma gets more contemplative and **retrospective** the older she gets.

memory word: red-troll-spectator

picture: A *red troll spectator* sits in the bleachers watching a basketball game. Every time the other team executes a free shot, he blares an air horn to distract them. Without fail, the fans in front of him *look back* at him in anger and frustration.

fondle: (**fon**-dl) **verb** – to handle or touch lovingly, affectionately, or tenderly

synonyms: caress, cuddle, embrace, nestle, nuzzle, pet, snuggle, stroke

example: Mom asks Junior, "Where's your dad?" He jokes sarcastically, "Where do you think? He's in the garage waxing and **fondling** his '76 Pontiac Grand Prix."

memory word: fawn-doll

picture: The Abominable Snowman is *petting* his new *fawn doll*, which Rudolph the Red-Nosed Reindeer got him for Christmas.

discerning: (dih-**sur**-ning) **adjective** – having or revealing keen insight and good judgment; quick to understand

synonyms: astute, insightful, judicious, perceptive, sagacious, shrewd

origin: From the Latin *discernere,* meaning "to set apart, distinguish."

example: "The person without the Spirit does not accept the things that come from the Spirit of God but considers them foolishness, and cannot understand them because they are **discerned** only through the Spirit."
(1 Corinthians 2:14)

memory word: dis-earning

picture: A little boy is born with dollar signs in his eyes. By age seven, he has a thriving franchise of lemonade stands, paper delivery routes, and other prosperous ventures. He tells all of the little boys and girls working for him, "Take pride in your work. Don't take handouts, and don't ***dis earning*** your own money." They think he is very *insightful*.

imprecate: (**im**-pri-kayt) **verb** – to invoke or call down evil or curses upon a person; to utter obscenities or profanities

synonyms: curse, damn, denunciate, execrate, maledict, swear

origin: From the Latin *imprecari*, meaning "invoke, pray, call down upon."

example: Have you ever heard the proverb "It is better to light a single candle than to curse the darkness"? If you want to impress someone you could say, "It is better to light a single candle than to **imprecate** the darkness." The proverb means that in the face of bad times or hopelessness, it is more worthwhile to do some good, however small, than complain about the situation.

memory word: imp-bra-Kate

picture: Kate is embarrassed by the imp standing on her shoulder wearing nothing but a bra. That's embarrassing enough, but the imp is *invoking curses* on all of her friends, who are a little creeped out by the *imp bra* on *Kate*'s shoulder.

resolute: (rez-uh-loot) **adjective** – firmly resolved or determined; set in purpose or opinion

synonyms: adamant, fixed, inflexible, settled, steadfast, unwavering

origin: From the Latin *resolutus,* meaning "dissolved, of loose structure."

example: CNN, an avowed "Never Trumper" organization, is **resolute** in its mission to bring President Trump down and have him impeached.

memory word: raise-yo-loot

picture: As the riot police march down the street toward the rioters and looters, the ring leader says to his gang of thugs, "We can beat these pigs! I have not yet begun to fight! If you're with me, *raise yo loot* and give me a rebel yell!"

relish: (**rel**-ish) **verb** – to take pleasure in; to like the taste of; to look forward to

synonyms: cherish, delight in, enjoy, go for, luxuriate in, revel in, savor

example: Many Asian cultures consider it a compliment to the cook if you slurp your soup and burp after a meal to show that you **relished** it.

memory word: relish

picture: While everyone else is *enjoying* hot dogs at a tailgate party, one man is feasting on a spicy *relish*. He likes *relish* so much that he is *savoring* it straight out of the jar.

incipient: (in-**sip**-ee-uhnt) **adjective** – beginning to exist or appear; in an initial stage

synonyms: commencing, embryonic, inceptive, inchoate, nascent

origin: From the Latin *incipere,* meaning "to begin, take up."

example: In the **incipient** stage of American football, players wore leather helmets.

memory word: ant-sip-ant

picture: A giant cannibalistic ant sprinkles half of the regular amount of ants into his hot cocoa, for today he *commences* a strict diet. It's creepy watching an ***ant sip ant**s*.

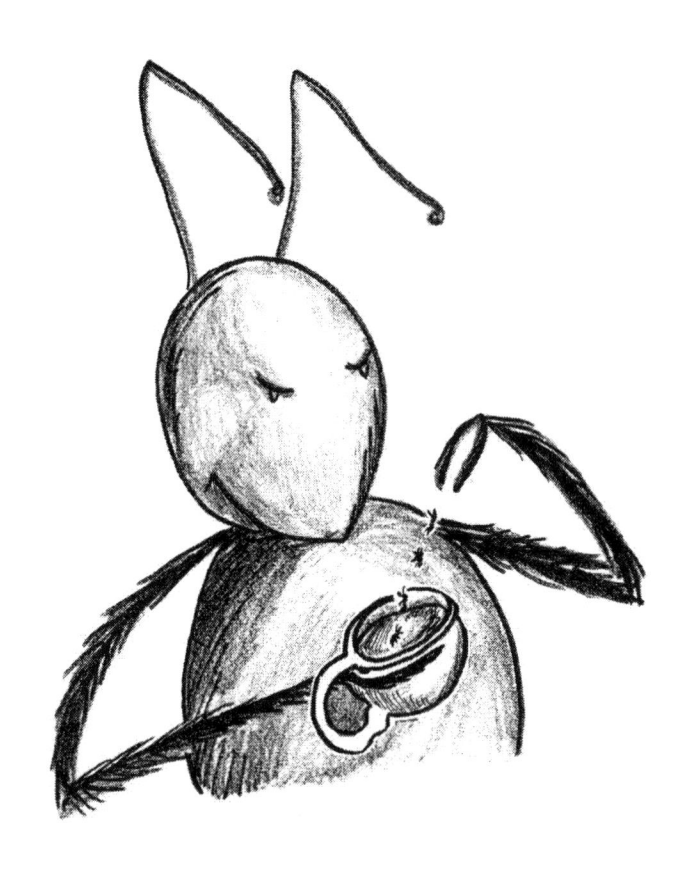

concede: (kuhn-**seed**) **verb** – to acknowledge as true, just, or proper; to admit defeat

synonyms: capitulate, cede, cry uncle, fold, give up, relinquish, surrender

origin: From the Latin *concedere,* meaning "to give way, yield."

example: The vote count was a nail biter, but eventually, the losing candidate had to **concede** defeat.

memory word: con-seed

picture: The escaped convict should never have taken that back country road. Listen to the hillbilly describe how he captured him . . . "Well, he aimed his little city-folk pea shooter what he wrangled from a guard. Me and my 13 kids pointed ours at his head and heart. The *con seed* he was outnumbered, so he throwed his hands up in the air and *surrendered*."

paltry: (pawl-tree) **adjective** – contemptibly small in amount; not worth considering

synonyms: insignificant, meager, measly, petty, piddling, worthless

example: In Luke 21:1–4, Jesus uses the story of the widow's donation of a **paltry** amount, as compared to the large donations of the wealthy, to explain to his disciples that the small sacrifices of the poor mean more to God than the large donations of the rich.

memory word: pole-tree

picture: When Werdnerd's friend's wife answers the doorbell, he asks, "Is your significant other around?" She says sarcastically, "You mean my *insignificant* other. Mr. **Worthless** is in the garage drinking beer and painting a pole green. He says we are going to have a ***pole tree*** for Christmas from now on."

undermine: (**uhn**-der-mahyn) **verb** – to sabotage or subvert in an underhanded way; to weaken or cause to collapse by removing underlying support

synonyms: debilitate, disable, erode, foil, impair, sandbag, thwart

example: Termites quietly and stealthily chomp and chew at the wooden frame in a house until they **undermine** the integrity of the whole structure.

memory word: under-mine

picture: A monkey comes home from work to find his tree (home) lying on the ground. Termites are feeding on what's left of the tree's roots. To his neighbors, he says, "Who knew those buggers were *weakening the foundation* of my house all this time? You monkeys better get yours checked for termites, too, because if they were *under mine*, they are probably under yours.

perspicacity: (pur-spi-**kas**-i-tee) **noun** – keenness of mental perception and understanding; discernment

synonyms: acumen, astuteness, cleverness, insight, shrewdness

origin: From the Latin *perspicere,* meaning "to look closely at."

example: Someone with **perspicacity** is good at looking for clues and coming to accurate explanations.

memory word: purse-pickaxe-a-T

picture: A huge crowd is celebrating Oktoberfest at the town square. A purse with *keen insight* is the only one noticing a letter T's suspicious behavior. When the T pulls out a knife, the purse pulls out her pickaxe and chases the T away. Thankfully, the *purse pickaxes a T* before it can harm anyone.

homogeneous: (hoh-muh-**jee**-nee-uhs) **adjective** – made up of parts or elements that are all of the same kind

synonyms: alike, comparable, consistent, identical, uniform, unvarying

origin: From the Greek *homogenes*, meaning "of the same kind."

example: The academic community has become a **homogeneous** bunch of group-thinkers. Over 90 percent vote for candidates who prefer socialism or communism over capitalism.

memory word: almost-genius

picture: A set of triplets are *identical.* Even their IQs are *exactly the same.* They're just one point below genius, which makes them *almost genius*.

juggernaut: (**juhg**-er-not) **noun** – a large, overpowering, destructive force or object, as in an army, earthmoving machine, undefeated football team, etc.

synonyms: colossus, monstrosity, steamroller, tank, unstoppable force

example: The U.S. government has morphed into a massive **juggernaut**.

memory word: jug-or-knot

picture: A *colossal* milk jug and a *monstrosity* of a rope knot face off for a death match. Which will overpower and destroy the other . . . the *jug or knot?*

opportunist: (op-er-**too**-nist) **noun** – a person who adapts his or her actions to take advantage of opportunities or circumstances, usually at the expense of morals and ethics

synonyms: carpetbagger, chameleon, timeserver, weathercock

example: Opportunistic politicians live by this statement by former White House chief of staff Rahm Emanuel: "You never want a serious crisis to go to waste; it's an opportunity to do things that you could not do before."

memory word: hop-tunist

picture: A consummate beer drinker just won the "Beer Drinker of the Year" award. (Yep, that's a real award.) He's unemployed and has few skills other than being an expert on all things beer. He discovers that a local brewpub is looking for a new brewmaster to brew the perfect beer. He *takes advantage of the only opportunity* available to him. He becomes the brewpub's *hoptunist*, tuning into just the right variety and amount of hops and malted barley to make the perfect beer.

ile: (**vol**-uh-tl) **adjective** – tending to break out into open violence; to fluctuate sharply and regularly; evaporating rapidly

synonyms: explosive, temperamental; capricious, erratic, unstable

origin: From the Latin *volatilis*, meaning "fleeting, transitory, flying."

example: Risk-averse individuals won't invest in the stock market due to its **volatility**.

memory word: volley-till

picture: A volleyball coach's mood *changes quickly and often*. One day, upset that his team can't volley the ball for very long, he orders them to *volley till* they drop. Thirty seconds later he screams, "Okay! Stop for ice cream!" While they're enjoying their break, he furiously overfills the volleyballs with the air pump, and then spikes them so hard they *explode*.

obeisance: (oh-**bay**-suhns, oh-**bee**-suhns) **noun** – bending the head, body, or knee as a sign of reverence, submission, shame, or greeting

synonyms: bow, curtsy, deference, genuflection, kowtow, prostration

origin: From the Latin *oboedire*, meaning "to obey; to pay attention to."

example: Grateful to be home, the returning POW performed a solemn **obeisance** immediately after disembarking the plane. He got down on all fours and kissed the tarmac.

memory word: obey-sons

picture: A domineering dad comes home from work and his five sons greet him at the door. They *bow* and keep their heads down as they say in unison, "Welcome home, Father. Our chores and homework are complete. What would you have us do now?" He says, "Very well. See how smoothly things go when you *obey, sons?*" The oldest says, "Yes, imperator, uh, I mean Father."

guile: (gahyl) **noun** – crafty or artful deception

synonyms: cunning, dishonesty, duplicity, treachery, trickery, wiliness

example: Despite his crafty **guile** and his absurdly complex contraptions, Wile E. Coyote never succeeded in capturing the guileless Road Runner.

memory word: guy'll

picture: It's Werdnerd's first day at a new school. A veteran student shadows him to show him the ropes. She points at a fox leaning against some lockers, saying, "Watch out for him. That *guy'll* steal you blind and convince you that you had it coming."

tutelage: (**toot**-l-ij) **noun** – the act of guarding, protecting, or guiding; instruction as from a tutor

synonyms: apprenticeship, coaching, education, guidance, training

origin: From the Latin *tutela*, meaning "a watching, protection."

example: Many high school students find higher level math very difficult. It is much more manageable under the **tutelage** of a college math major.

memory word: too-dull-edge

picture: A survivalist is teaching you and your friends how to survive in the wilderness. He inspects your hunting knife, advising, "It has a *too dull edge*." Then, he shows you how to sharpen it.

chastise: (**chas**-tahyz) **verb** – to discipline, especially by corporal punishment; to criticize severely

synonyms: flog, lash, punish, spank, whip; berate, castigate, upbraid

example: The doctor **chastised** his patient for not adhering to his diet and exercise regimen and for letting his cholesterol get out of control again.

memory word: chased-ice

picture: You open the freezer to find an ice cream fudge bar chasing the ice cubes around. What a mess! All of the ice and every surface is covered with fudge marks. You are irate and *berate* the fudge bar, asking why it *chased ice*. Then you *spank* the fudge bar with a popsicle stick.

malcontent: (mal-kuhn-**tent**) **noun** – a person who is chronically dissatisfied

synonyms: bellyacher, complainer, grumbler

example: Everyone knows a **malcontent**: He's the guy wringing his hands, just waiting to be offended so he can launch.

memory word: Mao-content

picture: The communist dictator/mass murderer, Chairman Mao, killed upwards of 80,000,000 of his people! His execution minister reported the execution numbers to Mao every day, asking, *"Mao Content?"* If Mao was *dissatisfied*, the execution minister had to double the numbers the next day.

servile: (**sur**-vahyl, **sur**-vil) **adjective** – slavishly submissive

synonyms: craven, fawning, obeisant, obsequious, sycophantic

origin: From the Latin *servilis,* meaning "of a slave."

example: A downward-spiraling economy and high unemployment tend to make employees more **servile,** because they want to please the boss and keep their jobs.

memory word: surf-aisle

picture: An employee at a general store in Hawaii hangs out in the *surf aisle* so he can meet the "cool surfers." After he assists surfers with a purchase, they always say, "thanks, dude." Then he bows, chanting, *"I'm not worthy,* dude. *I'm not worthy."*

facet: (**fas**-it) **noun** – a distinct element or feature in a problem; a smooth surface

synonyms: angle, perspective, position, situation, slant, view

origin: From the Latin *facies*, meaning "appearance, form, figure."

example: Not sure if she should change careers, she drew up a list of pros and cons and weighed every **facet** before she made a decision.

memory word: faucet

picture: The new *faucet* in your kitchen double sink extends too low into the sink and cannot swivel over the divider, into the other sink. This *distinct feature* is problematic.

catharsis: (kuh-**thahr**-sis) **noun** – the purging of the emotions or relieving of emotional tensions

synonyms: cleansing, expurgation, lustration, purging, purification

origin: From the Greek *catharsis*, meaning "purging, cleansing."

example: Laughing and crying both serve as **catharsis**.

memory word: cat-Thor-sis

picture: Thor, Werdnerd's sister's cat, has a magical ability to *ease one's emotional pain* just by sitting in one's lap. After a very stressful day at school, Werdnerd comes home emotionally distraught and asks his sister, "Can I borrow the *cat, Thor, sis*?"

pretense: (**pree**-tens) **noun** – pretending or feigning; a false show of something

synonyms: affectation, façade, faking, guise, masquerade, shtick, trickery

origin: From the Latin *praetensus*, meaning "false or hypocritical."

example: The senator displayed a **pretense** of remorse for his "poor choice of words" when referring to his opponent's supposed mob ties.

memory word: pretends

picture: A football player is known for his ability to head fake and *feign* going in one direction when he intends to go the other way. When the quarterback hands him the ball, he **pretends** there is something strange above by pointing to the sky and shouting, "Whoa! Look at that!" The defense looks up, allowing him to slip past with ease. Looking back, he taunts, "Monkeys always look! See ya in the end zone, sucka!"

calamity: (kuh-**lam**-i-tee) **noun** – a great misfortune or disaster; grievous affliction

synonyms: cataclysm, catastrophe, hardship, ruin, scourge, tribulation

origin: From the Latin *calamitas,* meaning "loss, disaster, misfortune."

example: Martha Jane Cannary's parents died when she was only 12 years old. She went on to carve out a reputation as a legendary folk hero who lived fast, drank hard, and lived life to the fullest in a man's world. Her rough and tumble life full of hardship and misfortune is most likely the reason she acquired the nickname of **Calamity** Jane.

memory word: clam-it-Eddy

picture: Eddy sees impending doom around every corner. When the school's fire alarm goes off one day, Eddy runs screaming from the building, shrieking, "Fire! Fire! We're all gonna die!" Principal Strickland rolls his eyes, grabs Eddy by the collar, and says, "***Clam it, Eddy.*** You're making a fool of yourself again. It's just the monthly fire drill."

extol: (ik-**stohl**) **verb** – to praise highly

synonyms: acclaim, applaud, eulogize, exalt, glorify, laud

origin: From the Latin *extollere*, meaning "to place on high, raise."

example: The word **extol** is usually followed by "the virtues of." For instance, vegans **extol** the virtues of chia seeds.

memory word: X-stole

picture: The little old lady *praised* Big Bird for returning her purse, which a big *X stole* from her as she walked down Sesame Street.

abate: (uh-**bayt**) **verb** – to reduce in amount, degree, or intensity

synonyms: decrease, diminish, ebb, reduce, subside, taper, wane

example: As soon as summer arrives in Phoenix, everyone starts counting the days until the brutal triple-digit temperatures **abate**.

memory word: a-bait

picture: An inventor builds an enormous mouse trap to hold hundreds of mice and creates *a bait* that attracts mice from miles away. One drop of stinky cheese extract placed in the mouse hotel is all it takes to persuade them to check in. His invention *reduces the number* of mouse traps needed since one mouse hotel will accommodate all of the mice within a city block.

lurid: (**loor**-id) **adjective** – causing shock or horror; pallid in color; shining with the red glow of fire seen through smoke

synonyms: ghastly, grisly, gruesome, horrid; ashen, pale; flaming

origin: From the Latin *luridus*, meaning "pale yellow, ghastly."

example: One of Werdnerd's pet peeves is stop-and-go traffic, which often occurs after a bad car crash. Rubberneckers can't turn away from the **lurid** scene.

memory word: lure-it

picture: A creepy looking man, standing next to you at the zoo, casts his rod and reel line in the direction of a baby seal. He hands it to you, saying, "Quick! *Lure it* up to the railing here and I'll club it with my bat." You run away in **disgust,** shouting, "That's **horrid**! You're **revolting**!"

idiosyncrasy: (id-ee-uh-**sing**-kruh-see) **noun** – a characteristic, habit, or mannerism that is peculiar to an individual

synonyms: eccentricity, foible, habit, oddity, peculiarity, quirk, trait

origin: From the Greek *idiosynkrasia,* meaning "a peculiar temperament."

example: Everyone knows that guy with the **idiosyncrasy** of ending his corny jokes with a verbal rim shot . . . ba dum tshh.

memory word: video-secrecy

picture: You just met your fiancé last week, and the wedding is already scheduled for next week in Las Vegas. One of your fiancé's friends slips you a *video* in *secrecy*, whispering, "Your fiancé has some *quirks* you should know about before you take the plunge."

rapport: (ra-**pohr**) **noun** – a relationship of mutual understanding or trust and agreement

synonyms: agreement, bond, concord, harmony, hitting it off, simpatico

example: Good salespeople know how to quickly establish **rapport** with customers.

memory word: re-pour

picture: Some children who just met at a birthday party are sitting around the kid's table *hitting it off* quite well. An adult holding a pitcher of Kool-Aid asks if they want more. The birthday boy says, "***Re-pour*** another round for my new friends."

knell: (nel) **noun** – the sound of a bell rung to announce a death or a funeral; a sound or sign announcing something's end, extinction, or failure

synonyms: peal, ring, signal, sound, summon, toll, warning

example: Many factors contributed to the decline and fall of the Roman Empire. The birth and spread of Christianity and the barbarian invasions were its final death **knells**.

memory word: nail

picture: A very large, yet otherwise ordinary *nail* is playing chess with the Grim Reaper in a church belfry. His job is to *ring* the *solemn bell* whenever someone dies. The Reaper gets a text letting him know someone's number just came up. He gets up to leave and tells Death *Nail* he'll call him to *ring the bell* as soon as he collects the soul of the dearly departed.

behemoth: (bih-**hee**-muhth) **noun** – a gigantic beast; anything of monstrous size or power

synonyms: beast, colossus, giant, goliath, leviathan, mammoth, monster

example: The federal government has become the very **behemoth** the Founding Fathers strove to prevent with constitutional checks and balances.

memory word: be-he-moth

picture: Your friend, histrionic about anything and everything, sees a *giant* moth-like creature swoop down in front of her. She asks, "***Be he moth?*** Be he butterfly? That is the question I ask of thee!"

oscillate: (**os**-uh-layt) **verb** – to swing or move to and fro, as a pendulum does; to vary or vacillate between differing beliefs, opinions, conditions, etc.

synonyms: alternate, pendulate, seesaw, sway, swing, teeter-totter

origin: From the Latin *oscillare,* meaning "to swing."

example: Unable to decide which boy to go steady with, she **oscillated** with her decision until she finally resorted to flipping a coin.

memory word: Oz-so-late

picture: Oz attends the state fair, where he *vacillates* over whether to enter the corn-on-the-cob eating contest. Finally, he flips a coin, and the answer is *yes*. Because he has taken so long to decide, however, he doesn't enter the contest until five minutes after it starts. Although *Oz so late*, his technique of quickly moving his head **back and forth** like an oscillating fan clinches the first place ribbon.

tranquil: (**trang**-kwil) **adjective** – free from commotion or tumult

synonyms: balmy, calm, gentle, halcyon, pacific, placid, serene, still

origin: From the Latin *tranquillus*, meaning "quiet."

example: Although a Category 5 hurricane can generate winds exceeding 150 miles per hour, its eye is **tranquil**.

memory word: train-quill

picture: A train rests on a giant quill floating on a lake. The water is so *placid* and *calm* that it looks like the ***train quill*** is lying on a sheet of glass.

goad: (gohd) **verb** – to prick or drive with, or as if with a goad, rod, or spur

synonyms: goose, harass, instigate, needle, prod, urge

example: The government's ever increasing **goading** in the form of incentives, penalties, and regulations, if not countered by "We The People," will ultimately lead to tyranny.

memory word: goat

picture: A cowboy mounts his horse-sized *goat* and digs his *spur*s into its sides, *urging* it to giddy-up. It bolts out from under him, causing him to back flip into a cactus.

idealistic: (ahy-dee-uh-**lis**-tik) **adjective** – having a strong belief in perfect standards and trying to achieve them, even when this is not realistic

synonyms: dreaming, impractical, quixotic, unrealistic, utopian

example: The young are energetic, imaginative, and **idealistic**; the old are tired, dull, and realistic.

memory word: I-deal-lipstick

picture: A dealer at a card table in a casino deals out assorted colors of lipstick instead of cards. One of the poker players says, "What's this? We can't play poker with lipstick. That's *impractical and unrealistic.*" The dealer responds, "*I deal lipstick.* Take it or leave it."

noisome: (**noi**-suhm) **adjective** – offensive or disgusting, as an odor; harmful or injurious to health

synonyms: fetid, foul, malodorous, nauseating, noxious, putrid, vile

example: An ogre is **noisome** in every sense of the word. Come to think of it, so is my senator.

memory word: noise-some

picture: A ginormous ear says to an equally large nose, "Wow! Did you hear that *noise some*where over in the next county? It sounded like an elephant flatulated." The nose replies, "I didn't hear a thing, but it *smells disgusting*."

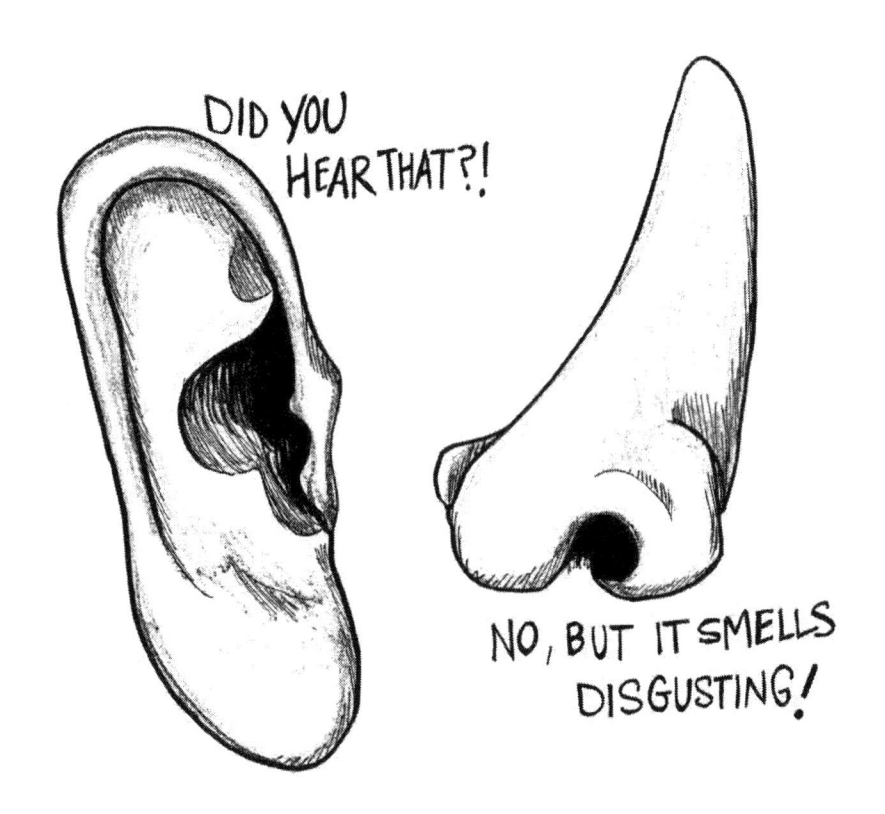

dynamic: (dahy-**nam**-ik) **adjective** – pertaining to or characterized by energy or effective action; vigorously active or forceful

synonyms: charismatic, electric, energetic, intense, magnetic, potent

example: Some believe that regardless of human emissions, the earth is in a state of **dynamic** equilibrium and mankind has no influence on the global climate.

memory word: die-in-hammock

picture: Everyone at work is shocked upon hearing the news that their most life-loving, *energetic, and vigorous* co-worker died over the weekend. You say, "Let me guess . . . his parachute didn't open? He fell into a volcano? He was gored to death while running with the bulls in Spain?" Someone responds, "Nope. Who would've thought he would *die in hammock* while taking a nap after church?"

pallid: (pal-id) **adjective** – pale or deficient in color; lacking in vitality or interest

synonyms: anemic, ashen, colorless, dull, wan; feeble, spiritless

origin: From the Latin *pallidus*, meaning "pale, colorless."

example: "Still **pallid** Death is knocking at the hovels of paupers and the towers of kings. O happy Sestius, the short span of life forbids us undertaking long hopes." — Horace

memory word: pow-lid

picture: Many containers of all shapes, sizes, and colors attend a Tupperware party. One of the containers says to a clear *colorless* lid standing alone, "Hey, pale face! What are you doing here? Go away! You don't belong!" Next thing you know . . . **POW! *Lid*** hauls off and punches the container right in the pie hole.

abscond: (ab-**skond**) **verb** – to depart in a sudden and secretive manner, especially to avoid capture and legal prosecution

synonyms: cut and run, duck out, escape, flee, hightail, make off, skip out

origin: From the Latin *abscondere*, meaning "to hide, put out of sight."

example: I have a T-shirt that says, "Run Like You Stole Something!" My laconic and sententious friend has a T-shirt that says, "**Abscond**!"

memory word: apps-gone

picture: You sit at your desk studying for an exam tomorrow, and you see movement out of the corner of your eye. You turn and are startled to see your app icons jumping off of your smartphone and *running away*. It's too late to do anything about it because *apps gone*.

morass: (muh-**ras**) **noun** – a tract of low, soft, wet ground; any confusing or troublesome situation, especially one from which it is difficult to free oneself

synonyms: marsh, quagmire; labyrinth, red tape, snarl, tangle, web

example: One lie leads to another and another until you find yourself entangled in an inescapable **morass**.

memory word: more-ass

picture: Two lizards warm themselves on a rock adjacent to some *quicksand*. They pass the time by keeping tabs on the number of animals that succumb to the *quagmire's* clutches. As a donkey walks into the quicksand, one of the lizards makes another mark on the rock saying, "Yet one *more ass*." The other lizard deadpans, "Yeah, I had a sinking feeling about that guy."

augment: (awg-ment) **verb** – enlarge in size, number, strength, or extent

synonyms: aggrandize, amplify, expand, increase, intensify, magnify

origin: From the Latin *augmentare*, meaning "to increase."

example: The president's State of the Union speech **augmented** the public's concern over his inability to lead and engendered a lack of confidence in his administration.

memory word: Og-mint

picture: The caveman scientist Og has succeeded in distilling the oil of mint leaves to the strongest, *most intense* extent possible. He instructs his lab assistant Neander to eat one of his mint chocolate chip cookies. The mint is so powerful it freezes Neander solid. Og muses, "I will have to wait for the Neander thaw (Get it?) before I can debrief him and find out what it felt like to consume the *Og mint*.

ornate: (awr-**nayt**) **adjectiv**e – elaborately decorated; over-embellished with rhetoric

synonyms: bedecked, elegant, gilded, jeweled, opulent; complex

origin: From the Latin *ornatus*, meaning "fitted out; adorned, decorated."

example: Cicero could write elegant verse just as easily as **ornate** prose.

memory word: Or-Nate

picture: Mrs. Brady asks her Literature Composition class to take turns reading aloud. After every student takes a turn, Mrs. Brady says, "Would someone like to read again? . . . *Or Nate*?" The class chants in unison, "Nate! Nate! Nate!" Nate is the class thespian who loves to *over-embellish*. Today he is *decked out* in his Shakespearean outfit and ready to play to the crowd.

dissident: (**dis**-i-duhnt) **noun** – a person who dissents or disagrees with an established policy, government, or authority

synonyms: agitator, heretic, nonconformist, protester, rebel, separatist

origin: From the Latin *dissidere,* meaning "to disagree, be removed from."

example: After winning the election, the president announced, "Now it's time to reward our supporters and punish the **dissidents**."

memory word: this-again

picture: The student body "representative" presents a list of demands to the principal. She says, "It's not fair that we don't have our own break room. We want a giant flat-screen TV, surround sound, Wi-Fi, free soda fountains, and a popcorn machine . . . non-negotiable. If we don't get what we want we go on strike." The principal rests his head on his hand, mumbling, "Not ***this again***."

chide: (chahyd) **verb** – to express disapproval of; to goad into action

synonyms: admonish, castigate, censure, reprimand, reproach, scold

example: Teenagers are often **chided** for not keeping their rooms clean.

memory word: chives

picture: The culinary school instructor *reprimands* a student for improperly cutting *chive*s. The instructor barks, "Step aside! I will demonstrate once more. Bunch them together like this. Push and slice them simultaneously like this. Or if you want just a little bit, take the scissors and cut them like this."

vivacious: (vahy-**vay**-shuhs) **adjective** – lively and animated

synonyms: bouncy, ebullient, sprightly, upbeat, vibrant

origin: From the Latin *vivere,* meaning "to live."

example: Every boy in school has a crush on the new girl. She's pretty, and she has a great sense of humor and a **vivacious** personality.

memory word: five-vases

picture: *Five vases* enjoy each other's company at the coffee shop. Each of them exudes an *ebullient and vibrant* energy. They gesticulate wildly while telling their stories. The laughter never stops.

mercurial: (mer-**kyoor**-ee-uhl) **adjective** – subject to sudden and unpredictable change

synonyms: capricious, erratic, fickle, flaky, impulsive, irregular, unstable

origin: From the Latin *Mercurius* (Mercury), the Roman god of travelers and commerce. Mercury was also the messenger of the gods.

example: Mercury's constant flying from place to place lends to **mercurial's** definition of unpredictability and flightiness.

memory word: Mercury-Al

picture: A thermometer high school reunion. A probe thermometer points across the room at a mercury thermometer and says to an infrared thermometer, "**Mercury Al** hasn't changed a bit. He's just as *emotional* as ever. Earlier I heard him *laughing*. A minute later he was *sobbing and lamenting* about how they are phasing out mercury-filled thermometers."

pervasive: (per-**vay**-siv) **adjective** – spread throughout

synonyms: omnipresent, permeating, ubiquitous, universal, widespread

origin: From the Latin *pervadere,* meaning "to spread or go through."

example: Corruption in D.C. is **pervasive**; the average politician accepts it as the way business gets done.

memory word: purr-invades-his

picture: A woman takes her husband to the doctor because he is starting to look and behave like a cat. After the doctor listens to his heart he laments, "I'm afraid he has cat scratch fever. There's nothing I can do for him once the *purr invades his* whole body."

inviolable: (in-**vahy**-uh-luh-buhl) **adjective** – secure from destruction, violence, infringement, or desecration; incapable of being violated

synonyms: invincible, sacrosanct, stable, unassailable, unbreakable

origin: From the Latin *inviolabilis*, meaning "invulnerable."

example: The U.S. Constitution is considered **inviolable** by conservatives. Progressives Leftists treat it as an outdated obstacle to progress.

memory word: in-vial-a-bull

picture: Right next to the "NO GUNS ALLOWED" and "NO SMOKING" signs on the front of a china store is a sign that says, "*IN VIAL A BULL* OR NO ENTRY." The owner will not allow a pet bull in her china shop unless it is contained in a vial. That way, her shop is *secure from destruction* by any loose bulls.

felicitous: (fi-lis-i-tuhs) **adjective** – well suited for the occasion, as an action, manner, or expression; marked by good fortune

synonyms: apropos, apt, fitting, germane, opportune; fortunate, lucky

origin: From the Latin *felicitas*, meaning "happiness, fertility."

example: Stories of government waste abound. Consider this example of a not-so-**felicitous** use of taxpayers' money: In 2013, the Department of the Interior spent $98,670 on a single toilet outhouse on an Alaskan trail.

memory word: Phyllis-it-is

picture: Phyllis has a large circle of friends who hold cocktail parties on a regular basis. She is known for her ability to say ***the right thing at the right time*** and is always the first to propose a toast. When Phyllis's friends hear the familiar sound of silverware tapping on a wine glass, they look for the source . . . and sure enough, ***Phyllis it is***. After getting everyone's attention, she utters the most ***appropriate*** benediction to the host and all in attendance.

exigent: (ek-si-juhnt) **adjective** – requiring immediate action or aid; requiring more than is reasonable

synonyms: critical, crucial, imperative, pressing, urgent; demanding

origin: From the Latin *exigere*, meaning "to demand, require; to drive out."

example: A politician's knee-jerk response to any **exigent** fiduciary crisis is to raise taxes and increase regulations.

memory word: exit-gent

picture: There is a large gathering of hundreds of wealthy women and one man in a conference center in a posh five-star hotel. The event's hostess takes the podium after a presentation and announces, "May I have your attention, ladies and gentleman. There is a Lamborghini Veneno (one of the world's most expensive cars) being towed from the parking lot. The owner might want to attend to this *urgent* matter." ***Exit gent!*** The gentleman bolts for the exit at lightning speed.

largess: (lahr-**jes**) **noun** – a generous bestowal of gifts; the gifts so bestowed

synonyms: altruism, philanthropy; beneficent, charity, endowment

origin: From the Latin *largus*, meaning "abundant."

example: The senator brings incredible amounts of federal **largess** to her constituents; consequently, she gets re-elected every six years.

memory word: large-S

picture: A *large S* stands next to a towering pile of gifts. The S *generously hands out gifts* to everyone who passes.

duress: (doo-**res**) **noun** – pressured to do something by threat or force; forcible restraint, especially imprisonment

synonyms: coercion, compulsion, constraint, pressure; detention

origin: From the Latin *durus,* meaning "hard."

example: If a politician tells the truth, you can bet he is under **duress**.

memory word: dress

picture: A schoolyard bully hands a cute little Easter *dress* to a boy, insisting, "You're gonna put this dress on and do a little dance so we can put it up on YouTube." The boy refuses until the bully gives him a wedgie and threatens to punch him in the nose and throw him in a locker. It's amazing how fast a little boy can figure out how to put on a dress!

gourmand: (goor-**mahnd**) **noun** – someone who eats good food to excess

synonyms: bon vivant, connoisseur, epicure, gastronomist, glutton

example: The difference between a **gourmand** and a gourmet is the quantity. A **gourmand** likes good food and wants to eat as much as possible. A gourmet likes good food, but doesn't overindulge.

memory word: gore-man

picture: A man who is *fond of good eating to excess* goes to the same restaurant every night and orders a thick, juicy steak in addition to the all-you-can-eat salad bar. He is known as The *Gore Man* because he prefers his steak very rare – in fact, oozing blood. He always jokes with the waitress, "If it ain't mooing, it's too done."

fraught: (frawt) **adjective** – filled with; accompanied by; marked by distress

synonyms: abounding, bristling, charged, full, replete, stuffed; burdened

example: Even though the whale ship was **fraught** with whale oil and ready to return home to Nantucket, the captain decided to chase after the great white whale. The crew knew this task was **fraught** with danger.

memory word: frog

picture: A corrupt career politician, who also happens to be a *frog*, is running for re-election. His campaign is crumbling because the media is doing its job, discovering that his administration is *filled with* scandals. They unearth a new one every week.

...BREAKING NEWS.... NEWEST FROG SCANDAL!!

putrid: (**pyoo**-trid) **adjective** – in an advanced state of decomposition and having a foul odor; morally corrupt, depraved, or evil

synonyms: decayed, fetid, malodorous, noisome, rancid, rank, rotting

origin: From the Latin *putrere,* meaning "to rot."

example: My representative is **putrid** in more ways than one. He reeks of B.O. and is morally and ethically corrupt.

memory word: pew-trick

picture: A preacher devises an ingenious way to keep his parishioners awake during his long sermons. He assigns a number to each section of every pew. When someone dozes off, he enters the seat number on the pad on his podium, and the seat releases a *foul, rotten egg odor* accompanied by a loud and realistic fart noise. It doesn't take long for the *pew trick* to train the chronic sleepers to stay awake.

coup: (koo) **noun** – a highly successful, unexpected stroke, act, or move; a sudden and decisive change of government illegally or by force

synonyms: overthrow, putsch, revolution, stratagem, takeover, upset

origin: From the Greek *kolaphos,* meaning "a slap, blow, or box on the ear."

example: Adolf Hitler's failed **coup**, The Beer Hall Putsch, landed him in prison for nine months in 1924. This attempt to seize power gained him national publicity . . . and the rest is history.

memory word: coo

picture: A six-month-old baby suddenly jumps out of his mom's lap in an *unexpected epic act*. He goes to the refrigerator, grabs a beer, and then goes into dad's study. He comes out chomping on a cigar and announces, "Listen up! The *coo* routine is over. There's only so much cooing I can stand. Oh, and while we're laying down some new rules, Pop, consider your *authority usurped*. I'll be sitting at the head of the table from now on . . . in my high chair, of course."

serendipity: (ser-uhn-**dip**-i-tee) **noun** – having good luck in making unexpected and fortunate discoveries by accident

synonyms: chance, dumb luck, fluke, fortune, happenstance, lucky break

example: In the late 1970s and early 1980s, Reese's Peanut Butter Cup commercials featured two people walking down the sidewalk minding their own business. One was eating a chocolate bar; the other was eating peanut butter. As they converged at a corner they collided, **serendipitously** discovering that chocolate and peanut butter were "two great tastes that taste great together."

memory word: Sarah-and-deputy

picture: Sarah says goodbye to her ex-boyfriend in prison. As she drives away from the prison, she prays that she will meet a law-abiding man, settle down, and start a family. A few minutes later, a deputy sheriff pulls her over for a broken tail light. It's love at first sight! He hands her a traffic ticket with the words "Will you marry me?" scribbled on the back. A few months later, ***Sarah and deputy*** are honeymooning in Fiji.

nostrum: (**nos**-truhm) **noun** – patent medicine whose efficacy is questionable; a medicine made by the person who recommends it; a scheme or theory supposed to remedy political or social problems

synonyms: curative, cure-all, elixir, panacea, quack medicine, snake oil

origin: From the Latin *nostrum remedium,* meaning "our remedy."

example: Politicians' **nostrum** for society's ills is bigger government.

memory word: nose-trim

picture: A career politician does his best *scheming,* er . . . I mean thinking, while trimming his nose hairs. Every time he does a *nose trim,* he comes up with an idea that he thinks will *solve society's problems* . . . and make him more powerful and wealthy.

idolatrous: (ahy-**dol**-uh-truhs) **adjective** – worshiping idols; blindly or excessively devoted or adoring

synonyms: adulatory, deified, heathen, pagan, romanticized

origin: From the Greek *eidololatria,* meaning "worship of idols."

example: The Holy Bible mentions **idolatrous** behavior many times. God's opposition to idolatry is included in the Ten Commandments: "You shall not make for yourself an image in the form of anything in heaven above or on the earth beneath or in the waters below. You shall not bow down to them or worship them." (Exodus 20: 4–5)

memory word: eye-doll-I-trust

picture: You are on your knees bowing to a big doll that has a giant eye for a head. You repeatedly chant, *"Eye doll I trust. Eye doll I trust."*

grievous: (**gree**-vuhs) **adjective** – causing grief or great sorrow; of great gravity or crucial import requiring serious thought; causing great pain or suffering

synonyms: agonizing, calamitous, egregious, grave, mournful, tragic

example: The thief suffered **grievous** injuries when he made the mistake of breaking into the home of the World Champion Marksman and NRA/GOA member.

memory word: grieve-us

picture: As a black widow spider courts a new lover, apparitions of her many past lovers appear, saying in unison, "*Grieve us*. *Mourn* us. Have you no *grief* for us?" The new lover says to her, "Yeah uh, I'm gonna have to take a rain check on our date. I just remembered I have a TPS report due on my boss's desk first thing in the morning. Gotta go. Bye."

toady: (toh-dee) **noun** – someone who tries to please another in order to gain favor

synonyms: bootlicker, brownnoser, doormat, lackey, minion

origin: Back in the day, mountebanks or snake oil salesmen would roll into town and use a toad eater to draw crowds and sell their quack medicine. Their assistant (**toady**) would eat a supposedly poisonous toad so the charlatan could then "expel" the poison, thereby "healing" the assistant with one of his nostrums. This disgusting job was done by one who would do anything to please his boss.

memory word: toady

picture: Todd, the toad, sits in the front row of a classroom full of lizards, amphibians, and toads. Every day he brings an apple to the teacher, Mrs. Goober, and compliments her attire. She always responds, "Oh, thank you, *Toady*. You're so sweet." The other students make fun of him, calling him "*Toady*," *goober smoocher*, *teacher's pet*, and other less than flattering names . . . except for the chameleon. He sits in the back row, stays quiet, and blends in.

nominal: (**nom**-uh-nl) **adjective** – insignificantly small; being such in name only

synonyms: minimal, small, token, trifling; so-called, supposed, symbolic

origin: From the Latin *nomen*, meaning "name."

example: Most apps are free; those that aren't usually have only a **nominal** cost.

memory word: Nam-and-all

picture: A soldier returns from the Vietnam War looking for a job, any job. He's willing to do any *trifling, insignificant* job, preferably one that will help him get his mind off of **Nam and all** its horrors.

preponderant: (pri-**pon**-der-uhnt) **adjective** – having superior power and influence

synonyms: dominant, overpowering, overriding, powerful, predominant

origin: From the Latin *praeponderare*, meaning "to outweigh."

example: The sun is by far the **preponderant** factor contributing to global warming or cooling. Humans are too insignificant to influence the earth's temperature one way or the other.

memory word: green-ponder-ants

picture: A classroom of ants in a critical thinking class sit in the "thinker pose." There are a few red ants and black ants, but the big ***green ponder ants*** outnumber, outweigh, and out-everything the others by a huge margin.

liability: (lahy-uh-**bil**-i-tee) **noun** – a hindrance or disadvantage that holds you back; something for which one is legally responsible

synonyms: baggage, drawback, handicap; arrears, damage, debt, IOU

example: A low SAT score is a **liability** if you have any hope of getting into a prestigious university.

memory word: lying-Billy

picture: Running from his mounting *debts*, Billy travels from town to town, never staying in one place for long. His most encumbering *handicap* is his inability to tell the truth. He lies so much that he is called *Lying Billy.*

iridescent: (ir-i-**des**-uhnt) **adjective** – having a play of lustrous rainbow colors

synonyms: opalescent, pearly, polychromatic, prismatic, shimmering

origin: From the Latin *iris,* meaning "rainbow."

example: Iris came to the Romans via the Greeks. In Greek mythology, Iris is the personification of the **iridescent** rainbow.

memory word: er-uh-desk-ant

picture: Werdnerd goes shopping for a new desk for his office at the Desk Depot. The salesman, an ant dressed like a hippie, is balding with a ponytail and wears a *rainbow* tie-dyed T-shirt, bell bottom jeans, and sandals. Werdnerd inquires, *"Er, uh, desk ant?* Why are you dressed like a hippie?"

debauch: (dih-**bawch**) **verb** – to corrupt morally by intemperance or sensuality

synonyms: debase, defile, demoralize, inveigle, pervert, seduce, warp

example: Way Cool Jr. came to town from somewhere down south. He partied all night and **debauched** all of the women with his sinful ways.

memory word: the-badge

picture: Your neighbors call the police to complain about the loud and wild partying at your house. When the police officer at your door sees all the food and drinks and the pretty women having a great time his eyes light up. You *seduce* him into joining the revelry. He accepts, but first you insist he must take off *the badge* because it will put a damper on the party.

cerebral: (suh-**ree**-bruhl) **adjective** – involving intelligence rather than emotions or instinct; relating to the brain

synonyms: analytical, brainy, erudite, intellectual, scholarly

origin: From the Latin *cerebrum*, meaning "brain."

example: The professor in this illustration is rather **cerebral** while wearing the bra on his head.

memory word: siree-bra

picture: A professor walks into the lecture hall on the first day of the semester wearing a pink polka-dot bra on his head. You lean over and ask a nearby student if that is indeed a bra on his head. The student says, "Yes, *siree. Bra* it is. Without it, he is as dumb as a bag of hammers, but once he straps that bra on his head, he's a regular Einstein!"

sedentary: (**sed**-n-ter-ee) **adjective** – characterized by sitting or resting a great deal

synonyms: desk-bound, inactive, sluggish, stationary, torpid

origin: From the Latin *sedere,* meaning "to sit."

example: Homer Simpson never exercises. He leads a very **sedentary** life.

memory word: sit-Aunt-Hairy

picture: The circus is in town! Your Aunt Hairy is The Bearded Lady. When she drops by to visit your family, you give her a big hug, invite her in, and say, "***Sit, Aunt Hairy***. Take a load off your feet."

beseech: (bih-**seech**) **verb** – to ask for or urgently plead

synonyms: adjure, appeal, beg, entreat, implore, petition, solicit

example: Werdnerd **beseeches** the bully, "Please. Take my lunch money. Take my cape. But *please* don't take my dictionary."

memory word: bees-each

picture: Two bees stand at a street intersection *begging* for money. The *bees each* have a cardboard sign stating they are down on their luck.

execrate: (ek-si-krayt) **verb** – to detest utterly; to curse or imprecate evil upon

synonyms: abhor, accurse, condemn, damn, excoriate, jinx, revile

origin: From the Latin *execrari*, meaning "to curse, hate, abhor."

example: The deplorable senator **execrated** anyone who opposed him in his quest for power and riches.

memory word: X-a-crate

picture: A voodoo witch doctor fears that the new doctor in town will take business away from her, so she marks an X on all of the crates containing his equipment and medicine. She believes that if she *X a crate*, it will *jinx* his practice.

intrigue: (in-**treeg**) **noun** – a crafty plot to achieve sinister ends; **verb** – to cause to be interested or curious

synonyms: ruse, scheme, stratagem; captivate, enchant, fascinate, pique

origin: From the Latin *intricare,* meaning "to entangle, confuse."

example: The phrase "**intrigue** killed the cat" doesn't have the same ring as "curiosity killed the cat."

memory word: in-tree

picture: A group of people stands under a tree. *Curious and captivated,* they gawk up *in tree* to catch a glimpse of the elephant trumpeting through its trunk.

attribute: (uh-**trib**-yoot) **verb** – to credit to; to ascribe to; (**a**-truh-byoot)

noun – a quality or characteristic given to a person, group, or other entity

synonyms: accredit, apply, impute; aspect, facet, feature, trait

origin: From the Latin *attributum,* meaning "anything attributed."

example: The **attribute** of the ten-gallon hat is **attributed** to Buffalo Bill Cody, who requested it be created larger than life for his Wild West Show.

memory word: hat-tribute

picture: A group of cowboy hats pays tribute to a ten-gallon hat, admiring it for its distinct *features*. They present it with a *hat tribute* trophy, which has ten miniature hats stacked one on top of the other.

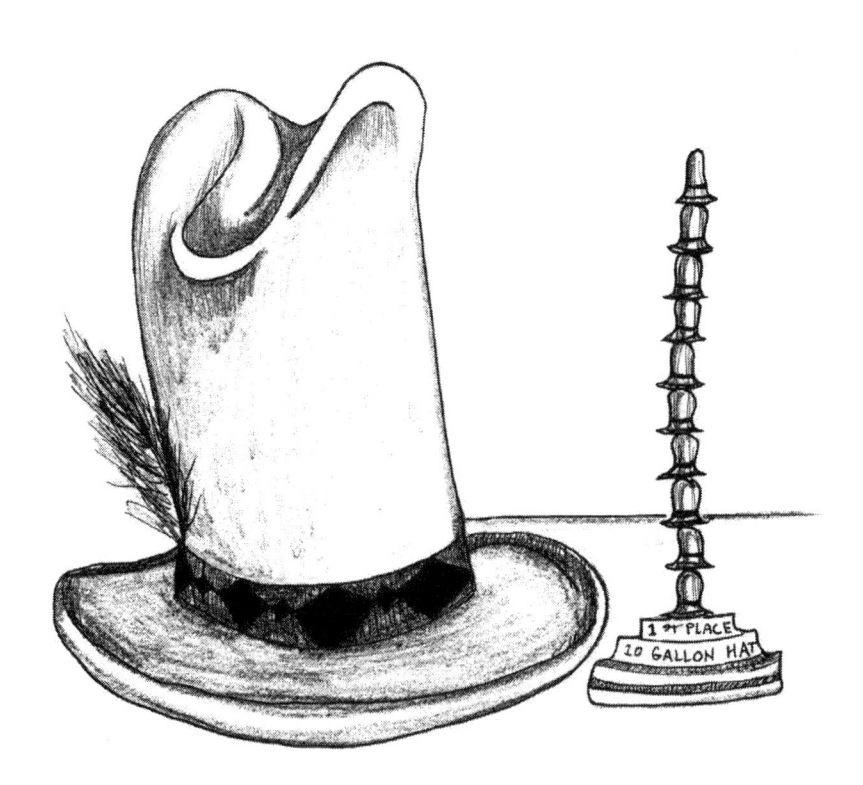

kismet: (kiz-met) **noun** – fate; destiny

synonyms: divine will, karma, lot, predestination

example: When their eyes met from across the crowded room, they both thought . . . **kismet!**

memory word: KISS-met

picture: It was *destiny* when the four members of *KISS met.* The day they came up with their legendary name, bass player and mastermind Gene Simmons suggested, "How 'bout Wicked Lester?" Their front man and lead singer, Paul Stanley, countered, "Too complicated. We gotta stick with one word. Let's **K**eep **I**t **S**imple **S**immons." The rest is Kisstory.

dawdle: (**dawd**-l) **verb** – to waste time; to take one's time; to move slowly

synonyms: amble, dilly-dally, lag, loaf, loiter, mosey, saunter, stroll

example: God bless those parents who don't rush their toddlers but instead let them **dawdle** and stop to smell the roses.

memory word: dot-oil

picture: Werdnerd takes Dot for a walk. Dot *takes his time*, stopping to sniff the dotted oil stains in every driveway. The **dot oil** fascination makes the walk *proceed very slowly*, but that gives Werdnerd time to peruse his pocket dictionary.

nexus: (**nek**-suhs) **noun** – a means of connection; a connected series or group; the core of a matter or situation

synonyms: center, connection, core, link, network, tie, union

origin: From the Latin *nexus,* meaning "that which ties or binds together."

example: Many believe there is a **nexus** between the mind, body, and soul.

memory word: neck-sis

picture: When Werdnerd's sister wears a high ponytail, he notices a plug on the back of her neck. He asks, "What the heck is that on your ***neck, sis?***" She responds, "Oh, that's just my neck plug – my ***connection*** to the matrix."

sanction: (**sangk**-shuhn) **verb** – to authorize, approve, or allow; to give consent; to ratify or confirm; to impose a penalty on; **noun** – a restriction, ban, or penalty

synonyms: bless, endorse, okay, permit, support; action, punishment

origin: From the Latin *sanctionem*, meaning "act of decreeing."

example: This word can be confusing since it can have opposite meanings depending on its use. I **sanctioned** my daughter's use of the car last night. But after she broke curfew and damaged my front bumper, I imposed a **sanction** on her.

memory word: sang-shun

picture: A community choir *allows* most applicants to join. They even *consent* to a horrible singer joining the choir, thinking he will improve in time. After he ruins one of their performances, however, they have to reconsider. After he *sang, shun* him they did. They *penalized* him and will not even consider letting him return until he takes some singing lessons.

encumber: (en-**kuhm**-ber) **verb** – to impede or hinder; to burden or weigh down

synonyms: block, hamper, handicap, obstruct, oppress, saddle, tax

origin: From the Latin *incombrare,* meaning "to barricade."

example: If only politicians weren't **encumbered** by that pesky Constitution, they could really put the screws to us.

memory word: incomer

picture: A very busy employee has three in/out trays on her desk. The "in" tray is labeled *incomer*, the "out" is labeled *outgoing*, and the third is labeled *just-shoot-me!* The outgoing tray is empty, but the *incomer* and just-shoot-me! trays are leaning towers of *burdening* work that needs to be completed ASAP.

oligarchy: (ol-i-gahr-kee) **noun** – a political system governed by a few people

synonyms: aristocracy, duarchy, diarchy, triarchy, gerontocracy

origin: From the Greek *oligarkhia,* meaning "government by the few."

example: I have told my kids more than once that our family is run by an **oligarchy** . . . rule by the few, or more accurately, rule by the two.

memory word: olive-car-keys

picture: A bunch of generic silvery car keys bow to a small group of olive green car keys. The *olive car keys* are their rulers.

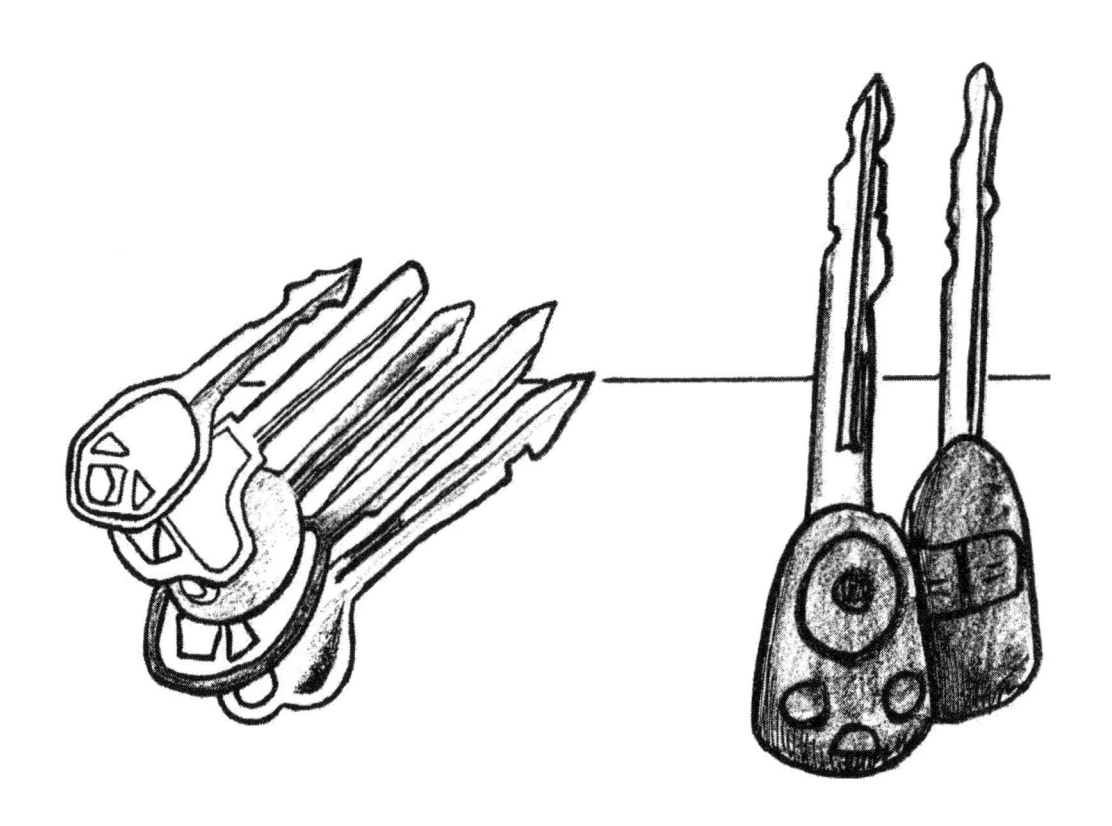

vagary: (**vay**-guh-ree) **noun** – an unexpected or erratic change in something; a whimsical, wild, or unusual idea, desire, or action

synonyms: caprice, impulse, inconsistency, notion, unpredictable, whim

origin: From the Latin *vagus,* meaning "roving, wandering."

example: Without snow-making machines, small-time ski resorts can be at the mercy of the **vagaries** of winter weather.

memory word: vague-Gary

picture: The weather guy on the evening news has earned the nickname *Vague Gary*. His forecasts are deliberately vague, so he can't be accused of being inaccurate. He always ends by saying, "It looks like there's a 50/50 chance of rain tonight; either it will or it won't. There's nothing more *unpredictable or erratic* than the weather."

appease: (uh-**peez**) **verb** – to bring to a state of peace, quiet, ease, calm or contentment; to satisfy, allay, or relieve

synonyms: assuage, conciliate, gratify, lull, mollify, placate, quell, soothe

example: Politicians subvert the Constitution behind the scenes and put on the face of **appeasement** for public consumption.

memory word: a-peace

picture: Jesus Christ appears in the midst of a group of angry protestors. His presence transforms the riotous energy of the entire group into a state of *peace and quiet*. Before vanishing, He flashes *a peace* sign.

pedagogy: (**ped**-uh-goh-gee) **noun** – the function or work of a teacher; the art or science of teaching

synonyms: edification, education, inculcation, indoctrination, instruction

origin: From the Greek *paidagogos,* meaning "teacher."

example: Great Hearts Academies is a network of state-chartered public prep schools in Metro Phoenix that believes in the **pedagogy** of a liberal arts education steeped in the rich tradition of Western civilization.

memory word: pet-a-goat?-Jeez!

picture: A wolf returns home after a long day of preying on goats and sheep. He discovers his wife and children petting their new pet goat. Throwing his hands up in the air in protest, he asks his wife, "Why would you *teach* the pups to *pet a goat? Jeez!*"

synchronous: (sing-kruh-nuhs) **adjective** – occurring at the same time

synonyms: coexistent, concomitant, concurrent, simultaneous

origin: From the Greek *synchronous*, meaning "happening at the same time."

example: The more **synchronous** lightning and thunder occur, the closer one is in proximity to the lightning.

memory word: sink-runners

picture: A couple of kitchen sinks run an exciting race. The *sink runners* tie, crossing the finish line *at the same time*.

resolve: (ri-**zolv**) **verb** – to come to a definite or earnest decision; to settle, determine, or state formally in a vote or resolution

synonyms: conclude, decide, decree, intend, propose, undertake, will

origin: From the Latin *resolvere*, meaning "to loosen, unyoke; to dispel."

example: Millions of people make a New Year's resolution to lose weight, **resolving** to cut calories and exercise more.

memory word: re-solve

picture: Werdnerd's teacher is disappointed because he can't solve a problem today that he could yesterday. She says, "You solved the very same problem 24 hours ago. C'mon, dig deep, *determine* you can do it and *re-solve* this equation."

bode: (bohd) **verb** – to be an omen of

synonyms: augur, forecast, foretell, herald, portend, predict, presage

example: The depravity and lack of morals and ethics of the modern politician do not **bode** well for the country's future.

memory word: bowed

picture: Little Werdnerd has an epiphany during a family reunion. Seeing his dad, grandpa, and great grandpa standing together, he realizes that each generation is more *bowed* over than the others. This awareness *portends* his poor posture in the future.

oblivious: (uh-**bliv**-ee-uhs) **adjective** – unmindful; unconscious; unaware (usually followed by *of* or *to*)

synonyms: absent, blundering, out to lunch, preoccupied, unobservant

origin: From the Latin *oblivion*, meaning "unaware, unconscious."

example: Werdnerd, engrossed in his dictionary, is **oblivious** to the commotion around him.

memory word: old-blivious

picture: A small geyser in Yellowstone National Park always erupts simultaneously with Old Faithful, which is just a few feet in front of it. Most tourists are *unaware* of ***Old Blivious,*** a pathetic little spit of water eclipsed by Old Faithful.

profuse: (pruh-**fyoos**) **adjective** – produced or growing in extreme abundance; made or done freely and excessively

synonyms: ample, bountiful, copious, lavish, plentiful, superfluous

origin: From the Latin *profundere,* meaning "to pour forth."

example: When the spelling bee monitor asked him to spell *vivisepulture,* Werdnerd's mind went blank, he broke into a **profuse** sweat, and he felt like he couldn't breathe.

memory word: pro-fuse

picture: The owner of the store Bombs 'R' Us is more of a fuse guy than a bomb guy. Only one aisle contains bombs, while the rest of the store contains an *abundance* of fuses. He's undoubtedly *pro fuse*.

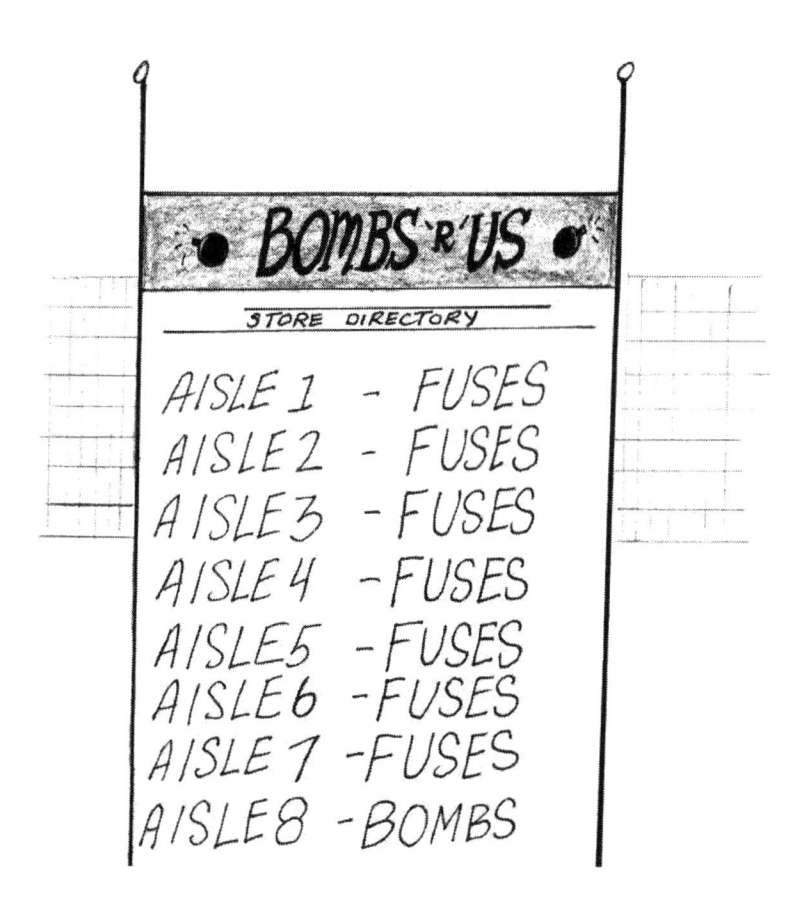

inundate: (in-uhn-dayt) **verb** – to flood or cover with water; to overwhelm

synonyms: deluge, drown, dunk, engulf, immerse, overflow, submerge

origin: From the Latin *inundare*, meaning "to overflow, run over."

example: The strange lights in the sky precipitated thousands of 911 calls, **inundating** the emergency call center.

memory word: N-on-date

picture: An N is on a date with a Q. The N is *overwhelmed* with questions from the Q. An ***N on** a **date*** with a Q should expect this.

avuncular: (uh-**vuhng**-kyuh-ler) **adjective** – resembling an uncle in kindness or indulgence

synonyms: benevolent, friendly, genial, helpful, tolerant

origin: From the Latin *avunculus,* meaning "maternal uncle"; literally, "little grandfather."

example: The **avuncular** pediatric dentist gently cautions the kids not to eat too many sweets, yet he sends each one away with a lollypop.

memory word: have-Uncle-Lars

picture: Dad is busy finishing up a project for work and can't break away long enough to take the kids to the baseball game, which they really, really want to see. He tells them to ***have Uncle Lars*** take them. Uncle Lars is more than happy to *indulge* his nieces and nephews.

excrescence: (ik-**skres**-uhns) **noun** – something that bulges out or projects from its surroundings; a normal or abnormal outgrowth of some part of the body

synonyms: accretion, growth; bone spur, carbuncle, lump, pimple, wart

origin: From the Latin *excrescentem*, meaning "abnormal growth."

example: A normal **excrescence** is hair or horns. An abnormal excrescence is a wart, a skin tag, or a bone spur.

memory word: X-crescents

picture: A huge X has large crescent-shaped *bone spurs* sticking out of its skin. The kids think the *X crescents* are cool.

temper: (**tem**-per) **verb** – to moderate or mitigate; to soften or tone down

synonyms: lessen, modulate, palliate, restrain, soften, take the edge off

origin: From the Latin *temperare*, meaning "to moderate, regulate, blend."

example: She **tempered** her critique of his speech with praise of its strong points.

memory word: temper (state of mind)

picture: Frankenstein is taking an anger management class to learn how to *moderate* his emotions, so that in the future he won't lose his *temper* and go on a rampage at the drop of a hat.

renegade: (ren-i-gayd) **noun** – a disloyal person who betrays or deserts his cause, religion, political party, friend, etc.; one who rebels and becomes an outlaw

synonyms: apostate, defector, deserter, traitor, turncoat; dissident, rebel

origin: From the Latin *renegare*, meaning "to deny."

example: Renegades who don't participate in strikes by their labor unions are called scabs.

memory word: rent-a-gate

picture: You quit your job at Gates 'R' Us and go to work at *Rent A Gate*. Your old boss considers you a *turncoat*.

ungainly: (uhn-**gayn**-lee) **adjective** – lacking grace in movement or posture; difficult to handle or manage especially because of shape

synonyms: awkward, clumsy, klutzy, uncoordinated, ungraceful

example: Werdnerd's dance instructor says she has never had such an **ungainly** student.

memory word: Nun-Gainly

picture: Sister Mary Gainly never seemed to grow out of her awkward tween stage. Because she is so *klutzy and ungraceful*, her students secretly refer to her as *Nun Gainly*.

quaff: (kwof) **verb** – to drink a beverage copiously and with hearty enjoyment

synonyms: down, gulp, guzzle, ingurgitate, swig, toss

example: Certain drinks can't be **quaffed** without pain. You'll burn your gullet with coffee if you don't sip it and you'll get a brain freeze if you **quaff** your Icee or Slushie.

memory word: go-off

picture: A giraffe goes into the bar at the same time every day. Unlike the other bar flies, who nurse their drinks, Mr. Giraffe *guzzles* his all at once and then lets out a horrendous burp after the *gulp* of booze sloshes down his long gullet. This disconcerting spectacle forces the bartender to strike an agreement with Mr. Giraffe. When he orders a drink, he must *go off* to a corner away from the other patrons and *down* his drink, burp, and then come back to join them.

satiate: (**say**-shee-ayt) **verb** – to fill to satisfaction; to make a pig of oneself

synonyms: cloy, glut, indulge, overeat, quench, sate, satisfy, slake

origin: From the Latin *satiare*, meaning "to fill full, satisfy."

example: An entire bucket of popcorn was required to **satiate** Werdnerd's craving.

memory word: say-she-ate

picture: After dinner, Grandma asks her granddaughter if she got enough to eat. She rubs her belly and burps so loudly the windows rattle. Grandpa says, "I'd ***say she ate*** all she can, Grandma."

bowdlerize: (**bohd**-luh-rahyz) **verb** – to expurgate by removing or modifying passages considered objectionable or indelicate

synonyms: black out, censor, delete, edit, redact, sanitize, strike out

origin: Thomas Bowdler is best known for publishing *The Family Shakespeare* (1807). He believed certain sexual references and double-entendres in the works of Shakespeare were not appropriate for women and children.

example: Thomas Bowdler wrote a **bowdlerized,** or expurgated, version of Shakespeare the whole family could enjoy.

memory word: bowled-her-eyes

picture: The recent discovery of a lost Grimm's fairy tale is exciting. However, its graphic nature warrants *censoring*. In the original version, an evil wizard rips out a giant woman's eyes and uses them as bowling balls. The *edited* version has him capturing a woman and using bowling balls tethered to her ankles with chains. The uncut version where he *bowled her eyes* is too gruesome for children.

necromancy: (**nek**-ruh-man-see) **noun** – a method of divination through alleged communication with the dead

synonyms: black art, occultism, sorcery, voodoo, witchcraft

origin: From the Latin *necromantia*, meaning "divination from an exhumed corpse."

example: Through **necromancy**, the witch conjured up the spirits of the dead and cast a spell on her enemies.

memory word: neck-rub-man-see

picture: A necromancer conducts a séance to summon a woman's deceased husband. After a few minutes, she motions toward the hazy crystal ball at the center of the table, declaring, "I'm seeing a man getting a massage. Yes! A *neck rub…man…see?* Do you see him?"

harbor: (**hahr**-ber) **verb** – to give shelter to; to conceal or hide; to hold in mind; **noun** – a sheltered body of water where ships can dock

synonyms: house, protect, quarter, safeguard, secrete; marina, port

example: Read *Letting Go* by Dr. David R. Hawkins if you want to learn how to let go of the negative emotions and feelings (anger, fear, jealousy, guilt, etc.) that we all **harbor**.

memory word: harbor (cove or inlet)

picture: A pirate ship *hiding* in a *harbor* from the British navy.

stupefy: (**stoo**-puh-fahy) **verb** – to put into a state of little or no sensibility; to benumb the facilities of; to put into a stupor; to overwhelm with amazement

synonyms: astonish, astound, bewilder, confound, daze, deaden, shock

origin: From the Latin *stupere,* meaning "to be stunned."

example: The Founding Fathers would be utterly **stupefied** if they were to witness the state of the union today.

memory word: stupid-fly

picture: A *stupid fly* repeatedly flies into a bug zapper. Over and over, he plops onto the floor and lies in a *stupor* for a minute or two. After regaining his senses, he flies into it again. And again. And again. And . . .

articulate: (ahr-**tik**-yuh-layt) **verb** – to utter clearly and distinctly; to pronounce with clarity

synonyms: enunciate, express, state, verbalize, vocalize

origin: From the Latin *articulare*, meaning "to divide into distinct parts; to utter distinctly."

example: If you memorize and use all of the words in the *Visualize Your Vocabulary* series, you will be able to **articulate** your thoughts very effectively.

memory word: R-tick-you-late

picture: A capital letter R is teaching a class of insects how to eliminate their stuttering and *speak clearly and distinctly.* When a tick arrives late to class, the *R* says, *"Tick! "You late!"*

incarnate: (in-**kahr**-nayt) **adjective** – embodied in flesh; given a human form; personified or typified, as a quality or idea

synonyms: alive, made flesh, manifested, materialized, substantiated

origin: From the Latin *incarnare,* meaning "to make flesh."

example: Werdnerd thinks he's so smart. Lately, he's been referring to himself as the dictionary **incarnate**.

memory word: in-car-Nate

picture: Nate was predestined to be the ultimate gearhead *in the flesh.* He was born in the back seat of a cab, with a wrench and screwdriver for hands. He was tinkering with cars in the garage alongside his dad before he could walk. Because he loved cars so much, he requested to be buried in his car. *In car Nate* was born . . . *in car Nate* was buried.

compliant: (kuhm-**plahy**-uhnt) **adjective** – obeying, obliging, or yielding, especially in a submissive way

synonyms: conforming, docile, meek, obedient, tractable, willing

origin: From the Latin *complir*, meaning "to accomplish, fulfill, carry out."

example: Wayne dreamed his teenage boys were perfectly **compliant**. What a rude awakening when they woke him up with a bull horn and a fire extinguisher!

memory word: come-fly-ant

picture: A termite calls a flying ant to come get him and drop him off at a party in the lumberyard. He barks, "*Come fly, ant!* Take me to the party, wait until I'm face down in sawdust, and then take me home. I'm gonna do hardwood shots till I pass out." The ant *obeys*, waiting for the inebriated termite until 3 a.m. and then flying him home.

quagmire: (**kwag**-mahyuhr) **noun** – an area of miry or boggy ground whose surface yields under the tread; a situation from which extrication is very difficult

synonyms: entanglement, jam, morass, pickle, pinch, predicament

example: When politicians get involved in military matters, the situation often turns into a **quagmire**.

memory word: quack-mayor

picture: A few months after electing a new mayor, the voters realize they have gotten themselves into a *predicament*. They start referring to him as the *Quack Mayor* for all of the lame-brained schemes he comes up with to solve the city's woes.

implacable: (im-**plak**-uh-buhl) **adjective** – not to be appeased, mollified, or pacified

synonyms: intractable, unbending, unforgiving, unyielding

origin: From the Latin *implacabilis*, meaning "unappeasable."

example: Nothing would pacify the **implacable** baby Werdnerd. When he was a toddler, his mom discovered that he could be content for hours while paging through a dictionary.

memory word: M-plaque-a-bull

picture: An M has offended a bull. It holds up a plaque that says, "I'm sorry. Please forgive me." The *M plaques a bull*, but the bull just stands there with his arms crossed. He is ***not easily pacified***.

boon: (boon) **noun** – something to be thankful for

synonyms: benefit, blessing, break, gift, godsend, good fortune

example: Rising oil prices are more of a **boon** to federal and state governments than to oil companies. The government's profit via taxes, from a gallon of gas, is seven times the oil company's profit! Remember that the next time you hear a politician demonizing "Big Oil."

memory word: boom

picture: Yesterday a military jet broke the sound barrier over a small town, creating a sonic *boom* that broke every window in town. This is a *godsend* for the town's only window repair business.

aspersion: (uh-**spur**-zhuhn) **noun** – a damaging or derogatory remark or criticism; the act of sprinkling water in baptism

synonyms: calumny, defamation, invective, libel, obloquy, slander

origin: From the Latin *aspergere*, meaning "to sprinkle on."

example: The quality of political debates has gone downhill with candidates casting **aspersions** back and forth.

memory word: at-Persians

picture: King Leonidas and his 300 bodyguards shouted *curses and derogatory remarks* at King Xerxes and his 300,000 Persians at Thermopylae. They knew it was suicide to hurl *invectives at Persians* of such a great number, but they also knew it would inspire the Greek city-states to unite and repel the Persian invasion.

penchant: (**pen**-chuhnt) **noun** – a strong inclination, taste, or liking for something

synonyms: affinity, fondness, leaning, partiality, predilection, proclivity

origin: From the Latin *pendere*, meaning "to hang, swing; to esteem."

example: Homer Simpson has a **penchant** for donuts.

memory word: pinch-ant

picture: The other ants can't stand the *Pinch Ant*, as they call him, because he has a *fondness* for pinching them.

vilify: (vil-uh-fahy) **verb** – to speak ill of

synonyms: defame, denigrate, denounce, malign, revile, slander, smear

origin: From the Latin *vilificare*, meaning "to make cheap or base."

example: Senator McLame **vilifies** anyone who disagrees with him.

memory word: Bill-if-I

picture: Two partners in crime are on opposite sides of a Plexiglas barrier that separates prisoners from visitors. Fashioning his hand into a gun, the prisoner says to his visitor, "**Bill, if I** hear you've been **talk'n trash** about me, it'll be the end of ya."

concomitant: (kon-**kom**-i-tuhnt) **adjective** – existing or occurring with something else, often in a lesser way

synonyms: affiliated, associated, attendant, connected, synergistic

origin: From the Latin *concomitari*, meaning "to accompany, attend."

example: Politicians don't seem to comprehend that when they increase taxes and regulations, there is a **concomitant** decrease in GDP.

memory word: con-comment-and

picture: A large and imposing con walks around the prison yard collecting protection money. Every time he makes a comment, his midget sidekick repeats the comment with emphasis or says, "Yeah! What he said!" The ***con comment*s, *and*** the midget parrots.

dissent: (dih-**sent**) **verb** – to disagree, especially with the majority, or with authority; to take an opposing view

synonyms: contradict, differ, object, oppose, protest

origin: From the Latin *dissentire,* meaning "to disagree, contradict."

example: The Boston Tea Party and the modern Tea Party both manifested to **dissent** against unresponsive and oppressive government.

memory word: this-end

picture: A contingent of aliens land on a dairy farm. They study a cow, trying to determine which end is the head so they can speak to it. All but one of the aliens is inspecting the hind end, concurring that it is the head. The alien at the cow's head *disagrees with the majority* saying, "Guys, I'm pretty sure *this end* is the head, because it smells considerably better."

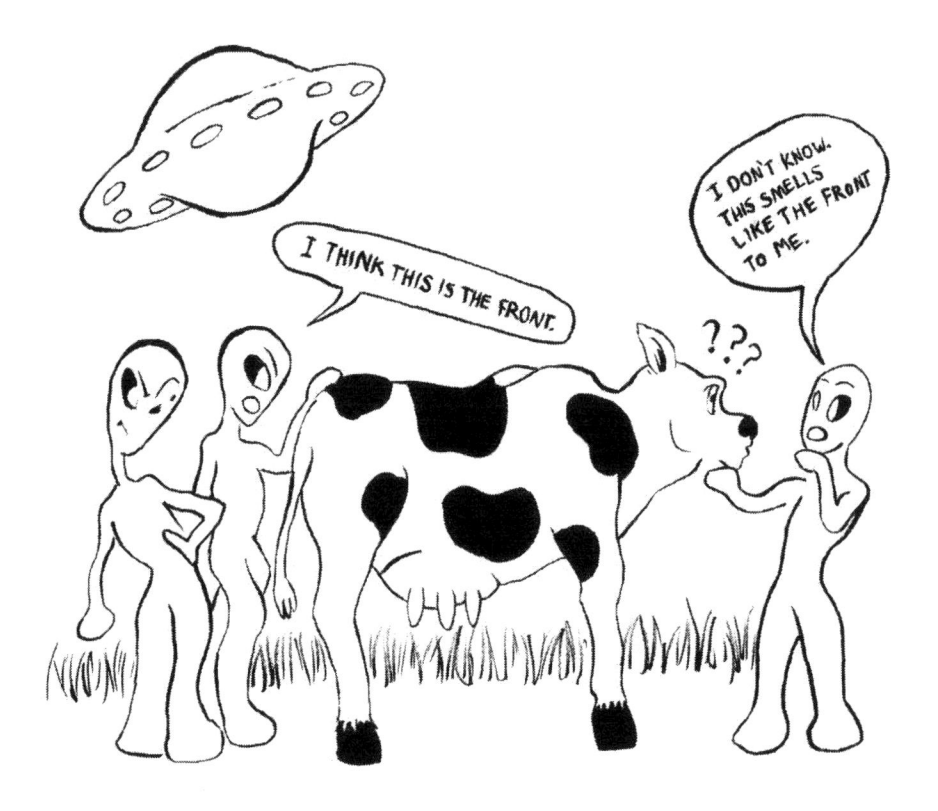

vicissitude: (vi-**sis**-i-tood) **noun** – a variation in circumstances or fortune at different times in your life or in the development of something; change; mutation

synonyms: fluctuation, reversal, shift, turnaround, ups and downs

origin: From the Latin *vicissitudinem,* meaning "change."

example: No one can escape the **vicissitudes** of life. We all have good times and bad times.

memory word: the-sissy-dude

picture: The behavior of the bipolar guy at school *alternates* drastically for no apparent reason. His classmates call him *The Sissy Dude* because one day he acts like a total sissy and the next day he's a cool dude.

opportune: (op-er-**toon**) **adjective** – occurring or coming at an appropriate time; appropriate, favorable, or suitable

synonyms: auspicious, convenient, felicitous, fortuitous, propitious

origin: From the Latin *opportunus,* meaning "fit, suitable, favorable."

example: When the cat's away, it's an **opportune** time for the mice to play.

memory word: opera-tune

picture: A guy is on a date with a promising prospect. He's nervous because he usually sticks his foot in his mouth, negating the possibility of a second date. He's on the verge of blurting out something offensive, but the fat lady at the table next to him stands up and belts out an *opera tune*. The fat lady sings *at just the right time* to save him from himself.

transmute: (tranz-**myoot**) **verb** – to change from one nature, substance, form, or condition into another

synonyms: metamorphose, mutate, transfigure, transform, transmogrify

origin: From the Latin *transmutare,* meaning "to transform."

example: Energy cannot be created or destroyed; it can only **transmute** from one form to another.

memory word: Fran's-mute

picture: Fran, a scientific genius, discovers how to *transform* base metals into gold, succeeding where thousands of alchemists throughout history have failed. When Werdnerd asks how she did it, her lab assistant responds, "Can't say." Werdnerd retorts, "Can't say or won't say?" The lab assistant says, "Can't say. *Fran's mute*."

furtive: (**fur**-tiv) **adjective** – taken, done, used, etc., surreptitiously or by stealth

synonyms: clandestine, covert, evasive, secretive, sly, sneaky

origin: From the Latin *furtivus*, meaning "stolen, hidden, secret."

example: Jill noticed out of the corner of her eye that Jack **furtively** wiped a tear from his cheek while watching the movie.

memory word: fur-tiff

picture: Mom and Dad Furball are raising the little Furballs to be peacemakers and never show any degree of upset. Whenever one of them needs to blow off some steam, he or she *sneaks* off and *secretly* throws a *fur-tiff*.

lucid: (loo-sid) **adjective** – easily understandable; transparently clear

synonyms: explicit, fathomable, limpid, unambiguous; translucent

origin: From the Latin *lucidus*, meaning "light, bright, clear."

example: Most of the time Grandpa is confused and doesn't make any sense; in his more **lucid** moments, however, it is obvious that he was a philosophy professor.

memory word: Lucy

picture: *Lucy* has a *transparent* skull which makes it easy to see her brain at work. That's what I call *clear thinking*.

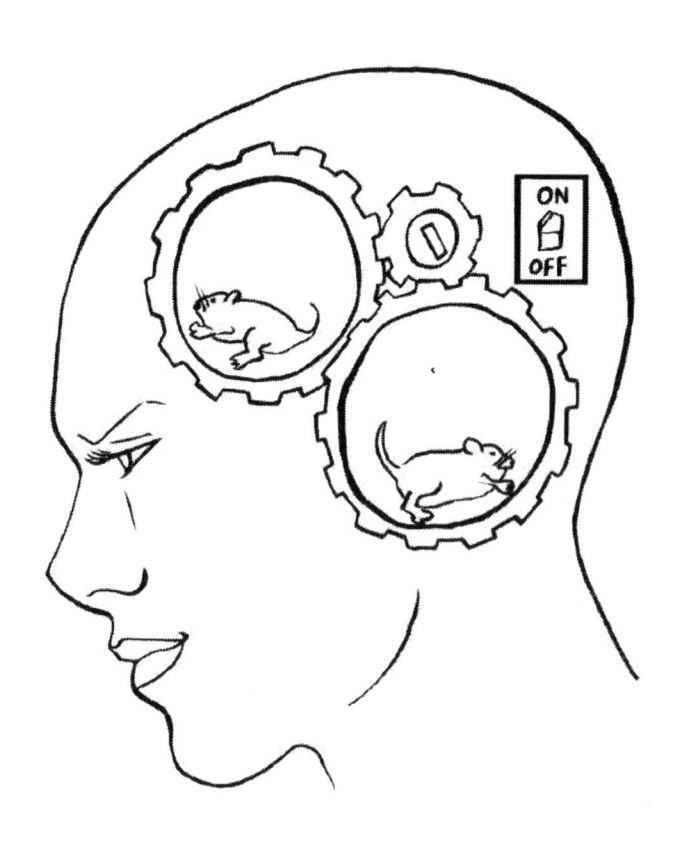

benediction: (ben-i-**dik**-shuhn) **noun** – an utterance of good wishes; the blessing at the close of a religious service

synonyms: blessing, grace, invocation, praise, sanctification

origin: From the Latin *benedicere*, meaning "to speak well of, bless."

example: When I drop my daughter off at school each morning, I send her away with a loving **benediction**: "Have a great day. Do your best. I'm proud of you. Good luck on your test."

memory word: Ben-addiction

picture: Werdnerd has a *Ben addiction*. He flies to London every weekend so he can spend a few hours gazing at Big Ben. Before he returns home each time, he says, "***Peace be with you,*** Ben. I *wish you well*. See you next weekend. ***God bless you!***"

viscous: (vis-kuhs) **adjective** – having a relatively high resistance to flow; thick and sticky

synonyms: gelatinous, gummy, gluey, gooey, slimy, syrupy

origin: From the Latin *viscosus,* meaning "sticky."

example: A lot of things that are **viscous** must be extracted by drilling. That goes for oil, maple syrup, or gooey boogers. The only one you should eat is the syrup!

memory word: discus

picture: The Diskobolus of Myron is a classical Greek *discus* thrower. The *discus* is filled with very **thick goo** that is ever so slowly leaking out, one *slimy* drop at a time.

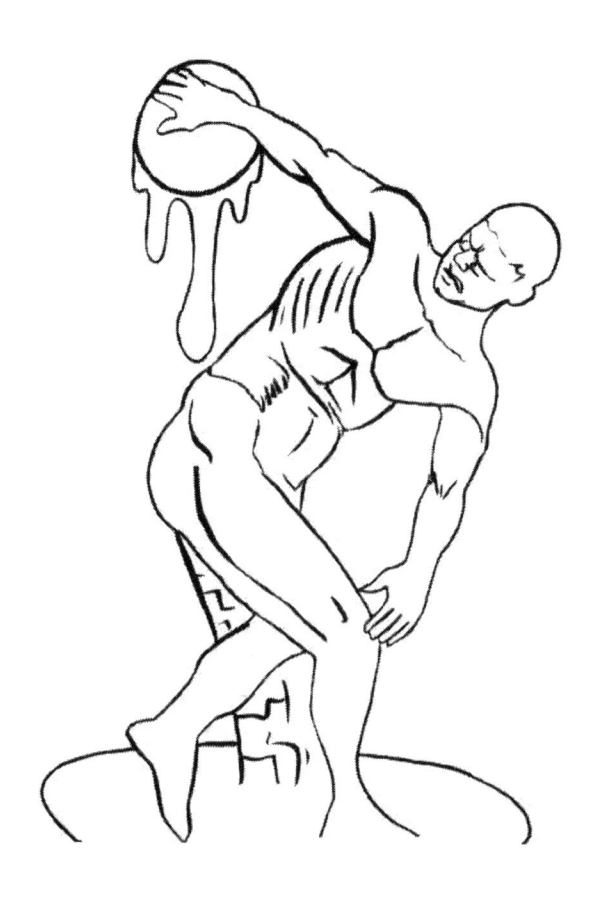

salient: (**say**-lee-uhnt) **adjective** – prominent or conspicuous; projecting or pointing outward

synonyms: outstanding, pronounced, remarkable, significant

origin: From the Latin *salientem*, meaning "leaping."

example: Some of George Washington's most **salient** qualities were virtue, honor, piety, and temperance.

memory word: sailing-ant

picture: A bunch of ants enjoy taking their sailboats out in the bay. One *sailing ant* has a sail twice as big as the others. It is *conspicuous* and stands out.

efface: (ih-**fays**) **verb** – to wipe out or do away with; to rub out, erase, or obliterate

synonyms: blot out, cancel, delete, destroy, eliminate, expunge, white out

example: A person with amnesia has had all or part of their memories **effaced.**

memory word: a-face

picture: An enormous pencil eraser comes out of nowhere and *erases* Werdnerd's face. What's a logomaniacal (word crazy) superhero supposed to do without *a face?*

rebut: (ri-**buht**) **verb** – to refute with evidence or argument; to prove to be false or incorrect

synonyms: controvert, disprove, invalidate, negate, overturn, repulse

origin: From the Latin *rebuter*, meaning "to thrust back."

example: To **rebut** something is the *act* of trying to prove it is false or incorrect. To refute something is the *result* of actually proving it.

memory word: red-butt

picture: Two big cigarette butts are on a stage debating whether or not smoking is hazardous to one's health. One is covered in red lipstick. The moderator tells the other butt it has two minutes to *disprove* the *red butt*'s argument.

circumscribe: (sur-kuhm-skrahyb) **verb** – to draw a line around; to enclose within bounds; to define limits

synonyms: confine, delineate, demarcate, encircle, hem in, limit, restrain

origin: From the Latin *circumscribere*, meaning "to make a circle around; to restrain, confine."

example: Laws serve to **circumscribe** the bad people rather than regulate the good ones.

memory word: circle-scribe

picture: A busy scribe tries everything he can think of to keep his 15 kids out of his work space. Finally, he builds a perfect circular trough around his work space, fills it with kerosene, and sets it on fire. The flaming *circle* the *scribe* built should do the trick. Or not?

predilection: (pred-l-**ek**-shuhn) **noun** – a tendency to think favorably of something in particular; propensity; proclivity

synonyms: bent, bias, fondness, partiality, penchant, preference

origin: From the Latin *prediligere*, meaning "to prefer before others."

example: The example for the word *penchant* (page 228) points out that Homer Simpson has a penchant for donuts. Well, he also has a **predilection** for Duff beer.

memory word: bread-election

picture: The world holds an election to determine which kind of bread is most popular. Russia has a *fondness* for rye, France is *partial to* the French baguette, Germany *prefers* the Kaiser roll, and Italy *favors* ciabatta. The *bread election* was as partisan as any other election. Go figure.

decadence: (dek-uh-duhns) **noun** – the act or process of falling into an inferior condition or state; moral degeneration or decay

synonyms: decline, degeneracy, gluttony, regression, sybaritism

origin: From the Latin *decadere,* meaning "to decay."

example: It is a wonder the **decadence** of ancient Rome didn't lead to its decline earlier than it did.

memory word: deck-dents

picture: A pool deck needs refurbishing. Many chips, dents, and flakes of cool decking reveal the concrete underneath. The ***deck dents*** indicate massive ***decay and decline***.

fetid: (fet-id) **adjective** – having an offensive odor; stinking

synonyms: gross, malodorous, putrid, rank, reeking, rotten, smelly

origin: From the Latin *fetere,* meaning "to have a bad smell, stink."

example: My college roommate frequently did the smell test on his pile of dirty laundry. If it wasn't too **fetid**, it was wearable.

memory word: fed-Ed

picture: You could always tell when Ed's mom fixed his favorite meal. The day after she *fed Ed* cabbage and nine bean soup, he produced an *offensive odor*.

variegated: (vair-ee-i-gay-tid) **adjective** – varied in appearance or color; marked with different shades, spots, patches of color; distinctly marked

synonyms: dappled, flecked, kaleidoscopic, mottled, multicolored

origin: From the Latin *variegare*, meaning "to diversify with different colors."

example: A male peacock spreads his **variegated** and extravagant feathered tail to impress potential mates.

memory word: very-gated

picture: You live in a *very gated* community. You pass through one gate only to enter a different pass code for the next gate, and the next, and the next. Each gate is a *different color* and is *distinctly marked*.

yield: (yeeld) **verb** – to give forth; to produce or furnish; to give up or in

synonyms: bear, bring in, harvest, profit; acquiesce, defer, surrender

example: The farmers were very happy with the **yield** of their crops this harvest.

memory word: yield (sign)

picture: A farmer proudly looks out at his bumper *crop* of *yield* signs.

dissolution: (dis-uh-**loo**-shuhn) **noun** – the act or process of dissolving into parts or elements; the undoing or breaking of a bond, tie, union, partnership, assembly, etc.

synonyms: breaking up, disintegration, disunion, divorce, separation

origin: From the Latin *dissolutionem*, meaning "a dissolving, destroying."

example: The **dissolution** of the ego reveals the spirit within.

memory word: this-solution

picture: A mad scientist stands before an assembly of other scientists. He pours liquid from one beaker into another beaker with liquid. Then he announces, "You have exactly one minute to clear out of this room before ***this solution*** goes KABOOM!" Needless to say, the assembly ***broke up*** immediately.

rampant: (**ram**-puhnt) **adjective** – unrestrained and violent; unchecked growth

synonyms: epidemic, out of control, pandemic, rampaging, widespread

example: Corruption is **rampant** in Washington, D.C.

memory word: ram-pant

picture: Some rams are going retro by wearing bell bottom jeans. Unfortunately, this fashion trend is *widespread and unrestrained*. Every day the bell bottoms of the *ram pants grow bigger.*

ominous: (om-uh-nuhs) **adjective** – signaling that something unpleasant is about to happen; portending evil or harm

synonyms: baleful, ill-boding, inauspicious, threatening, warning

origin: From the Latin *ominosus*, meaning "full of foreboding."

example: I should have paid more attention to these **ominous** signs: A black cat crossed my path, and I stood under a ladder that was leaning against a broken mirror.

memory word: almond-dust

picture: A squirrel has a penchant for almonds rather than acorns. He has squirreled away thousands of almonds for the winter. He cracks open one almond after another, only to find that each shell is empty except for a little bit of ***almond dust***. Mr. Squirrel thinks to himself, "Uh Oh! This **portends** a long, hungry winter."

DICTIONARY

MAKE A PICTURE OF IT. IT'LL LAST LONGER.
WN
Thesaurus
VISUALIZE YOUR VOCABULARY
DICTIONARY

About the Author

Shayne Gardner is a former history teacher who constantly encouraged his students to develop a strong vocabulary. He put a new word on the whiteboard every day and quizzed the students every Friday. The students who turned the words into pictures, as instructed, aced the quizzes every week.

Shayne lives with his wife and daughter in Chandler, Arizona. He would prefer to reside in Hawaii, so please purchase several copies of this book and gift them to family and friends.

VisualizeYourVocabulary@gmail.com

Facebook.com/VisualizeYourVocabulary

Pinterest.com/SATwerdnerd

Twitter.com/ SATwerdnerd

Google.com/+VisualizeYourVocabulary

Index

abate	148	bowdlerize	217
abduction	102	braggadocio	28
abhor	11	burnish	23
abjure	50	buttress	103
abscond	161	calamity	146
acrimony	26	calumny	52
adjure	51	captious	32
admonish	59	catharsis	144
adroit	3	cerebral	189
anathema	41	chastise	140
antagonist	1	chide	166
appease	202	circumscribe	242
apposite	106	cogent	55
aptitude	15	compliant	223
archaic	118	concede	129
arrogate	81	concomitant	230
articulate	221	coup	178
aspersion	227	criteria	114
atone	71	dawdle	196
attribute	194	debauch	188
augment	163	decadence	244
avuncular	210	demean	79
badger	49	derisive	24
balm	78	detrimental	10
banal	6	didactic	53
bearing	83	discerning	124
behemoth	153	discrepant	48
benediction	237	dissent	231
beseech	191	dissident	165
bleak	42	dissolution	248
bode	206	dissonant	21
bombard	68	diverse	107
boon	226	duress	174

Index

dynamic	159		imminent	120
efface	240		impecunious	92
egotist	60		implacable	225
egregious	8		imprecate	125
embellish	111		impromptu	110
encumber	199		incarnate	222
equivocate	19		incipient	128
eradicate	100		infallible	95
erstwhile	105		insolent	30
excoriate	66		intrigue	193
excrescence	211		inundate	209
execrate	192		inviolable	170
exigent	172		iridescent	187
existential	98		irrelevant	22
extol	147		juggernaut	134
facet	143		kismet	195
felicitous	171		knell	152
fetid	245		largess	173
filibuster	94		lavish	88
foil	61		legitimate	113
fondle	123		liability	186
forlorn	12		libel	72
fractious	20		lithe	14
fraught	176		loathsome	17
furtive	235		lucid	236
garrulous	25		luminary	40
goad	156		lurid	149
gourmand	175		malcontent	141
grievous	182		malefactor	58
guile	138		manifold	70
habituate	87		maudlin	54
hamper	4		meager	108
harbor	219		meander	39
homogeneous	133		mercurial	168
idealist	69		minutia	7
idealistic	157		misconstrue	116
idiosyncrasy	150		miscreant	56
idolatrous	181		morass	162

Index

narcissistic	34	pragmatic	90
necromancy	218	predilection	243
negate	45	preponderant	185
nexus	197	prerogative	97
nocturnal	93	prescient	13
noisome	158	pretense	145
nominal	184	proclivity	9
nostrum	180	procure	82
nugatory	37	profuse	208
nuisance	121	putrid	177
obeisance	137	quaff	215
objective	76	quagmire	224
oblivious	207	qualitative	85
oligarchy	200	query	109
ominous	250	rambunctious	31
onerous	44	rampant	249
opportune	233	rapport	151
opportunist	135	rebut	241
optimist	117	relish	127
ordeal	67	renegade	213
ornate	164	renown	89
oscillate	154	repertoire	73
ossify	101	replete	43
oust	84	resolute	126
pallid	160	resolve	205
paltry	130	retrospective	122
paradox	46	salient	239
pare	62	salubrious	38
pedagogue	35	sanction	198
pedagogy	203	satiate	216
peevish	18	sedentary	190
pellucid	91	seditious	27
penchant	228	serendipity	179
perplex	99	servile	142
perspicacity	132	slander	119
pervasive	169	somatic	86
piquant	80	spontaneous	2
platitude	112	stultify	65

Index

stupefy	220
subjective	77
supercilious	29
sybaritic	104
synchronous	204
tangent	63
taper	75
temper	212
terse	5
toady	183
tranquil	155
transmute	234
transpire	115
tutelage	139
umbrage	33
unctuous	57
undermine	131
ungainly	214
vagary	201
vagrant	96
variegated	246
vicarious	64
vicissitude	232
vilify	229
vintage	74
viscous	238
vitriolic	16
vituperative	36
vivacious	167
volatile	136
winnow	47
yield	247

Made in the USA
San Bernardino, CA
05 February 2018